Real China:
The Communist Party and
the People's Liberation Army
under Xi Jinping

解密中國：
習近平統治下的共產黨與解放軍

Radio Taiwan International
財團法人中央廣播電臺

**Facing the New International Landscape:
What You Need to Know from "Real China:
The Communist Party and the People's Liberation Army
under Xi Jinping"**

/ Radio Taiwan International Chairperson Cheryl Lai

According to statistics published in March 2024 by the V-Dem Institute at the University of Gothenburg in Sweden, Taiwan has ranked first for eleven consecutive years as the country most severely affected by foreign attacks. This dates back to November 2012, when Xi Jinping assumed the position of General Secretary of the Chinese Communist Party. Through various institutional means of centralizing power, Xi has strengthened personal dictatorship internally and pursued authoritarian expansion externally, affecting regional stability and international order, with Taiwan being the primary target. Besides direct military threats that heighten regional tensions, Xi uses hard-to-detect "grey zone" tactics to influence Taiwanese society. Recently, the most common method has been disinformation attacks using large-scale generative AI and content farms, coupled with local collaborators working in concert, making Taiwan, situated in a strategically critical geographic location in East Asia, the most severely attacked country in terms of cognitive warfare globally.

Radio Taiwan International (Rti), with its 96-year history, is a national public media outlet with expertise in international communication and multilingual proficiency. In response to the rapid changes in global geopolitics and the spread of disinformation, Rti's contemporary mission is to deliver accurate news to the world and report on the free and democratic voice of Taiwan.

In early 2024, to enhance international news reporting and communication capabilities and strengthen media resilience in interpreting news and situations related to China, we established a new department: Rti Academy. With strong support from the National Development Council's bilingual policy, we launched courses such as the "International Communication Talent Training Program" and "Media Resilience." We also published this manual, "Real China: The Communist Party and the People's Liberation Army under Xi Jinping."

This manual is designed for journalists, political workers, and all citizens concerned about Taiwan's security issues. It analyzes China's sharp power actions against Taiwan and the operational model of the Chinese Communist Party. Through straightforward courses and this manual, we aim to enhance the accuracy of media reporting on cross-strait issues and deepen public confidence in self-defense.

Additionally, Rti is dedicated to multi-platform broadcasting, boasting numerous international loyal listeners through podcasts, the internet, and shortwave broadcasts. Bearing the mission of Taiwan's voice, Rti not only responds to the global media's demand for Taiwan-related reports but also aspires to leverage its multilingual expertise to provide Taiwan's perspectives and experiences. Rti seeks to provide the Taiwanese perspective and experience to more foreign media stationed in Taiwan and the growing immigrant community, enhancing Taiwan's visibility internationally and strengthening the affinity of local foreigners towards Taiwan as a democratic partner.

Partnering with global media counterparts is both an obligation and a mission for Rti as a national broadcaster. Protecting the quality of democracy and our beautiful homeland is the responsibility of all Taiwanese people. Let's start with this manual, "Real China: The Communist Party and the People's Liberation Army under Xi Jinping," to build and strengthen the resilience of our entire society's defense!

面對國際新局，你所需要的
《解密中國：習近平統治下的共產黨與解放軍》

/ 財團法人中央廣播電臺　賴秀如董事長

根據瑞典哥德堡大學「多元民主中心 V-Dem」2024 年 3 月公布的統計顯示，台灣連續 11 年蟬聯榜首，是全球遭受境外攻擊最嚴重的國家。時間回溯至 2012 年 11 月，正是習近平出任中國共產黨中央總書記。他透過諸多制度性集權手段，對內強化個人獨裁，對外進行威權擴張，衝擊區域安定與國際秩序，台灣更是首當其衝。除了直接軍事恫嚇，升高區緊張局勢，更利用難以辨識的「灰色地帶」戰術，影響台灣社會。近來最慣用手法，就是以大規模生成式 AI 與內容農場的假訊息攻擊，配合在地協力者裡應外合的唱和，讓身處東亞戰略關鍵地理位置的台灣，成為全球受認知戰攻擊最嚴重的國家。

已經有 96 年歷史的中央廣播電臺（Radio Taiwan International，Rti），面對假訊息充斥與全球地緣政治的快速變化，身為兼具國際傳播、多語專業的國家公共媒體，向國際傳遞正確新聞，報導自由、民主的台灣之聲，就是 Rti 央廣的當代使命。

2024 年初，為提升國際新聞編採與傳播能力，增強對中國新聞與情勢判讀的媒體韌性，我們成立了新部門：央廣學院（Rti Academy），以因應種種內外部挑戰。在國發會雙語政策的大力支持之下，我們開設「國際傳播人才培訓計畫」與「媒體韌性」等課程，也出版這本《解密中國：習近平統治下的共產黨與解放軍》手冊。

這是一本為新聞從業人員、政治工作者與所有關心台灣安全的公民所編寫，解析中國對台灣的銳實力行動與中國的黨政運作模式的實務手冊。透過深入淺出的課程與手冊，盼能提升媒體在兩岸議題報導的精準度，也深化民眾自我保衛的信心。

此外，Rti 央廣致力於多平台傳播，在播客、網路與短波廣播中，擁有眾多國際忠實聽眾。肩負台灣之音使命，Rti 央廣呼應國際媒體對台灣報導需求的同時，也期許未來能發揮多語種專業，提供台灣觀點與台灣經驗，服務越來越多的駐臺外籍媒體與新住民群體，提高台灣在國際的能見度，深化在臺外籍人士對台灣這個民主夥伴的向心力。

與全球媒體夥伴們攜手並進，是央廣身為國家廣播媒體的義務與使命。守護民主品質與我們的美麗家園，則是全體台灣人民的責任。現在就跟著這本《解密中國：習近平統治下的共產黨與解放軍》手冊，一起構築強化全體社會防衛韌性的工程吧！

Reference link for analyzing disinformation attacks
假訊息攻擊分析參考連結

Content
目錄

Chapter 1

A battledfield without gunpowder: China's influence operations against Taiwan — 07
沒有煙硝的戰場：中國對臺灣影響力行動

1-1 The invisible blade: an introduction to China's influence — 08
隱形的刀刃：簡介中國影響力

1-2 China's influence revealed: Chinese tourists and China's financial operations in Taiwan — 11
影響力現形：陸客觀光與臺商

1-3 China's influence revealed: China's propaganda and disinformation operations in Taiwan — 16
影響力現形：媒體宣傳背後的中國銳實力

1-4 Signal flares in the fog: information manipulation and information literacy — 26
迷霧裡的信號彈：資訊操弄與資訊判讀

1-5 Out of the foggy battlefield: case studies of China's information manipulation against Taiwan — 30
走出迷霧戰場：中國對臺資訊操弄案例

Chapter 2

Through the red lens: an analysis of the CCP's political operations — 47
紅色透視鏡：中共政治運作解析

2-1 The mysterious Chinese government & party organizations — 48
紅色神秘的中國政府與黨組織

2-2 Evolution of a dictator: Xi's institutional centralization of power — 56
獨裁者的進化：習近平與制度化集權

2-3 The dilemma of dictators: succession crisis in the red empire — 64
獨裁者的兩難：紅色帝國接班危機

Chapter 3

Dismantle the PLA's attack plans for Taiwan: PLA's military operations against Taiwan — 71
破解解放軍攻臺策略：共軍對臺軍事行動

3-1 Understand your enemy, yourself, and your surroundings: intelligence preparation of the battlefield, IPB — 72
知天知地、知己知彼：戰場情報準備

3-2 Taiwan's defense tactics: battlefield advantages and strategic challenges — 74
臺灣防衛的憑藉：戰場優勢與策略挑戰

3-3 The ground force, navy, air force + PLA's rocket force: introduction to the PLA — 82
陸海空＋火箭軍：解放軍軍隊介紹

3-4 Maritime or airborne warfare: How will the PLA initiate the war? — 90
海上來還是天上來：解放軍怎麼打？

Source 資料來源 — 93
Acknowledgments 致謝 — 95

Chapter 1

A battlefield without gunpowder: China's influence operations against Taiwan
沒有煙硝的戰場：中國對臺灣影響力行動

Authoritarian countries' use of disinformation and cognitive warfare to expand outward, posing a threat to democratic countries, has been a rising issue in recent years. According to a report from the University of Gothenburg in Sweden, Taiwan has ranked as the number one target of foreign disinformation attacks for eleven consecutive years. Media outlets such as Agence France-Presse (AFP) have set up fact-checking sections on their websites to combat spreading fake news. As a national media outlet broadcasting in multiple languages, Radio Taiwan International (RTI) is committed to joining forces with the global democratic alliance to counter cognitive warfare. Therefore, the first unit is titled "A Battlefield Without Gunpowder: China's Influence Operations Against Taiwan." Also, we invited Jaw-Nian Huang, associate professor of the Graduate Institute of Development Studies at National Chengchi University, and Josh Wang, CEO of the Taiwan Information Environment Research Center, to share their insights for this unit.

Disinformation and cognitive warfare are also defined as "influence operations" by the RAND Corporation, a U.S. defense think tank. In this course, participants will learn about the three models of China's influence operations, understand why authoritarian countries are motivated to use sharp power to influence Taiwan and delve into the most intriguing case studies. Additionally, participants will learn how to debunk China's information manipulation through the "Information Credibility Assessment." By the end of this unit, participants will have a clear understanding of the information manipulation tactics of authoritarian countries and be able to analyze the intentions and goals of the CCP's information operations.

Keywords: sharp power, local collaborators, information manipulation, information credibility assessment

威權國家利用假訊息和認知戰向外擴張，造成民主國家的危害，是近年的新興議題。在瑞典哥德堡大學的研究報告中，臺灣是連續十一年，名列遭受境外假訊息攻擊第一名的國家；各國媒體如法新社（Agence France-Presse，AFP），就在官網頁面設置事實查核專頁，對抗假訊息的氾濫。央廣做為以多語傳播的國家媒體，肩負和世界民主同盟攜手對抗認知戰的義務，因此把「沒有煙硝的戰場：中國對臺灣影響力行動」放在第一單元。也邀請政大國發所黃兆年副教授，以及臺灣資訊環境研究中心王希執行長，來講解這個單元。

假訊息和認知戰，也就是美國國防智庫 RAND Corporation 定義的「影響力行動」。在本課程中，學員會學到中國影響力行動的三個模式、知道威權國家最有誘因使用銳實力來影響臺灣，以及大家最好奇的案例解說，與破解中國資訊操弄的「訊息可信度評量」。相信讀畢本單元後，對威權國家的資訊操弄模式會有清楚認識，也能深入分析中共資訊操弄的意圖與目標。

關鍵字：銳實力、在地協力者、資訊操弄、訊息可信度評量

1-1
The invisible blade: an introduction to China's influence
隱形的刀刃：簡介中國影響力

The definition of "influence operations"
「影響力行動」定義

What is an influence operation? An influence action involves the interaction of at least two actors, where actor A uses certain methods to influence the behavior or cognition of actor B, thereby achieving the goals that actor A hopes to accomplish. Therefore, this involves the relationship between means, objective, and means.

什麼是影響力行動呢？影響力行動，涉及兩個以上行為者的互動，其中行為者 A 用一些方法去影響行為者 B 的行為或認知，以此達到行為者 A 希望達成的目的。因此，這裡涉及的是目標、目的跟手段之間的關係。

Sources of China's influence
中國影響力的來源

How did China's influence operations occur? After 1978, China transitioned to a policy of reform and opening up, integrating into the global economic division of labor and trade systems. Starting as the world's factory and market, China continued to attract global capital. By the 2000s and 2010s, it began to become a capital-exporting country and a major financier globally. Through its different roles in the global economy, China has been able to exert significant influence worldwide through economic channels.

American scholar David Shambaugh interprets China's influence as "partial power," meaning that China's influence is not balanced across all areas. China has strong influence in the economic field, but relatively less influence in technology, diplomacy, military, and cultural areas.

中國的影響力行動是怎麼發生的？中國於 1978 年後轉向改革開放，鑲嵌進全世界的經濟分工跟貿易體系之中，從世界工廠與市場開始，持續吸納世界資金。到了 2000 年至 2010 年代，中國成為資本輸出國，成為世界的金主。中國透過在世界經濟裡頭扮演的不同角色，讓它可以循著經濟市場的管道，對全世界發揮一定的影響力。

美國學者沈大偉 David Shambaugh 將中國影響力理解為 partial power（局部強權），也就是說，中國在各方面的影響力並不均衡。中國在經濟的場域中有強大的影響力，相對於此，他在科技、外交、軍事、文化的層面上，對全世界的影響並不像經濟場域那樣顯著。

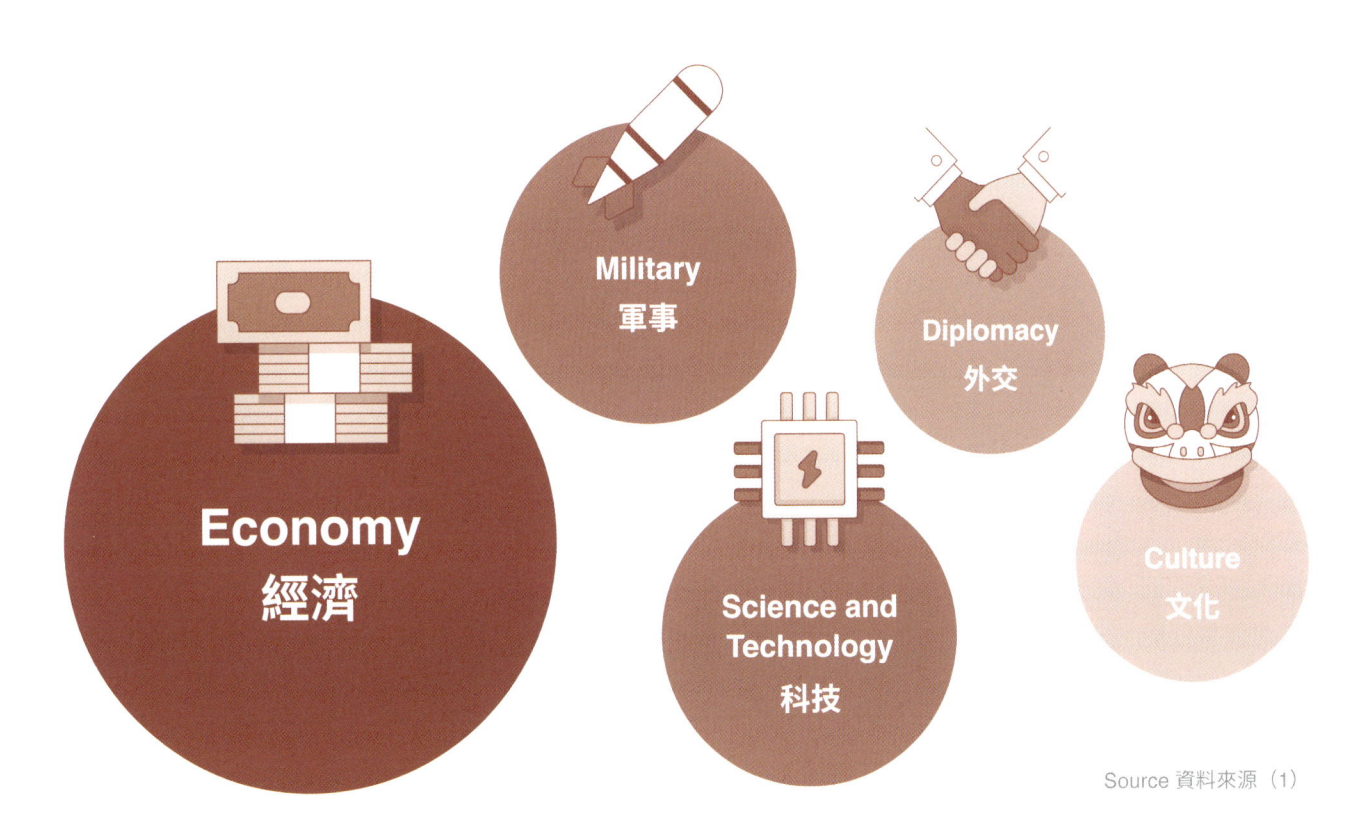

Source 資料來源（1）

Influence operation models:
an analytical framework of the China factor
for cross-strait relations context
影響力運作模式：兩岸關係脈絡－中國因素分析架構

According to the theoretical framework "China Factor" proposed by Jieh-min Wu, the Institute of Society, Academic Sinica, and based on the experience of cross-strait relations, we are going to introduce the two mechanisms by which China's influence exerts its influence on the outside world.

引用中研院社會所的學者吳介民在兩岸關係的經驗基礎上所提出的「中國因素」理論框架，帶大家認識中國影響力對外施展影響力的兩種作用力機制。

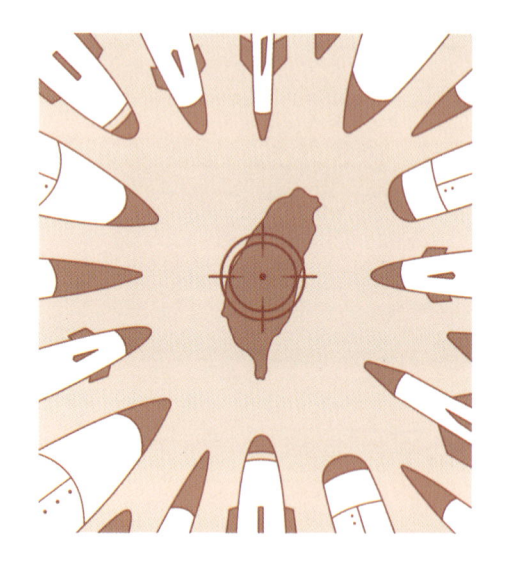

Direct influence is very straightforward. For example, during Taiwan's first presidential election in 1996, the missile crisis caused by China was an attempt by China to exert direct influence to affect the voting behavior of the Taiwanese people.

直接施力非常直觀，就是中國政府可以直接的對台灣發揮他的影響力，例如 1996 年台灣第一次民選總統時面臨的中國飛彈危機，就是中國運用直接施力，影響台灣人民投票行為的操作。

Indirect influence means that China exerts influence through intermediary channels. In this model, there are two important intermediary channels: the "Cross-strait Government-business Network" and the "Local Collaborator Networks." China exerts its influence, indirectly promoting Beijing's desired political objectives in Taiwan.

間接施力的意思是，中國透過中介的環節，間接影響台灣。在這個模式下有兩個重要的中介環節，一個是「跨海峽政商關係網絡」，一個是「在地協力者網絡」，間接的在台灣宣傳北京希望達到的政治目標。

1-2
China's influence revealed: Chinese tourists and China's financial operations in Taiwan
影響力現形：陸客觀光與臺商

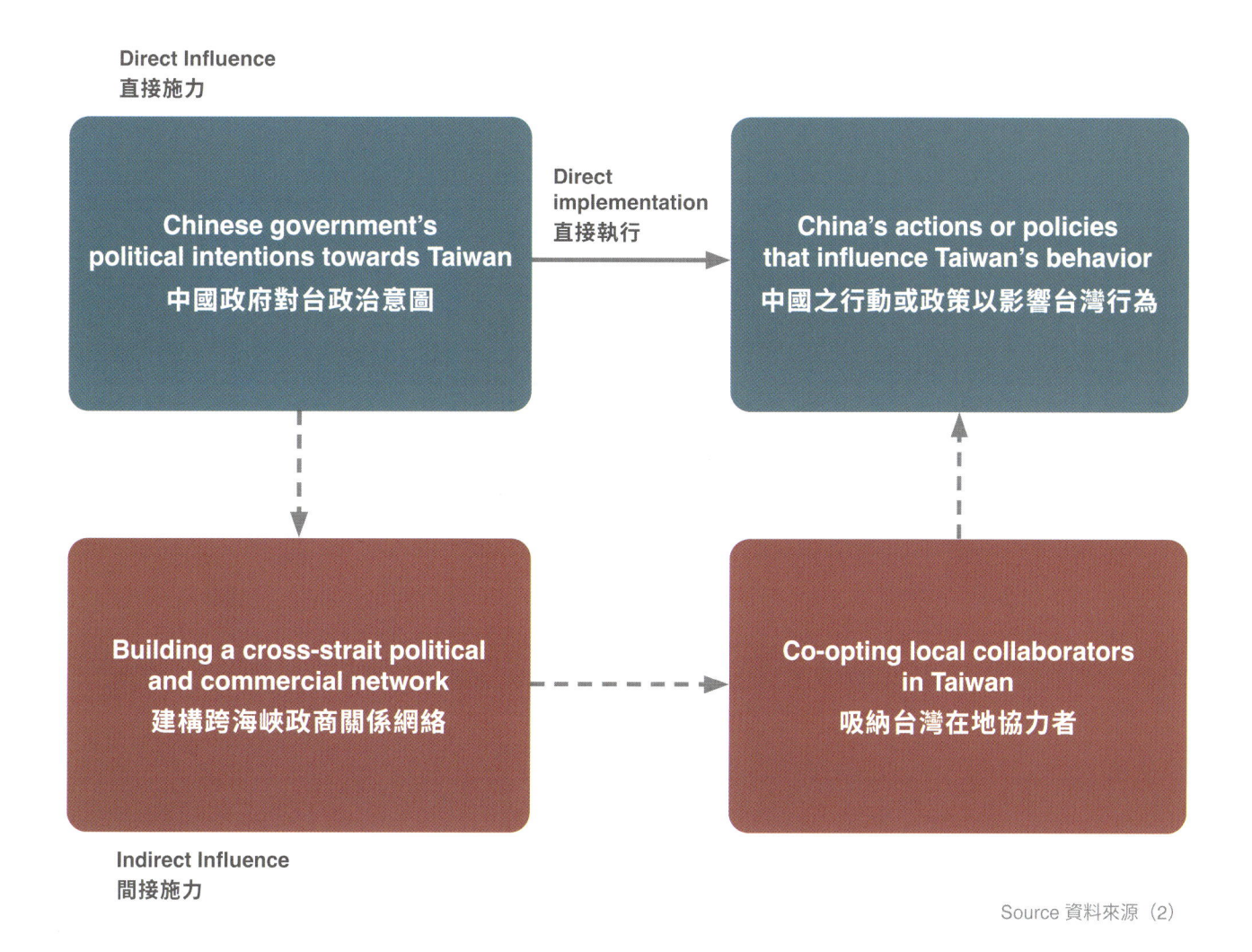

Direct Influence
直接施力

```
┌─────────────────────────┐   Direct        ┌─────────────────────────┐
│ Chinese government's    │   implementation│ China's actions or      │
│ political intentions    │   直接執行  ───▶│ policies that influence │
│ towards Taiwan          │                 │ Taiwan's behavior       │
│ 中國政府對台政治意圖      │                 │ 中國之行動或政策以影響台灣行為│
└───────────┬─────────────┘                 └─────────────▲───────────┘
            │                                             │
            ▼                                             │
┌─────────────────────────┐                 ┌─────────────────────────┐
│ Building a cross-strait │                 │ Co-opting local         │
│ political and commercial│ ─ ─ ─ ─ ─ ─ ─ ─▶│ collaborators in Taiwan │
│ network                 │                 │ 吸納台灣在地協力者        │
│ 建構跨海峽政商關係網絡    │                 │                         │
└─────────────────────────┘                 └─────────────────────────┘
```

Indirect Influence
間接施力

Source 資料來源（2）

Compared to the straightforward nature of direct influencein influence operations, indirect influence is more challenging to identify due to its intermediary stages. Therefore, in this section, we will analyze two practical cases to decipher China's indirect coercion models in influencing Taiwan. These cases involve Mainland Chinese tourists and local collaborators among Taiwanese businesses.

相較於影響行動中，直接施力的模式十分直觀好辨識，間接施力因為經過了中介環節，較難辨識，因此在這個單元，我們會透過兩個實際案例，解析中國對台影響力操作的間接施力模式。
這兩個案例，一個是陸客觀光，另一個則是台商的在地協力。

Chapter 1 | A battlefield without gunpowder: China's influence operations against Taiwan
沒有煙硝的戰場：中國對臺灣影響力行動

Trade dependence and local collaboration: Chinese tourist sightseeing
貿易依賴與在地協力：陸客觀光

1999
China first proposed the 1992 Consensus.
中國首次提出九二共識

2005
Lien Chan visited China and initiated cooperation between the KMT and the CCP.
連戰訪中開啟國共合作

2008
China started to allow tourists to visit Taiwan.
中國開放陸客來台

1996
Lee Teng-Hui won the first presidential election.
首次總統大選李登輝勝選

2000
The first political party alternation with Chen Shui-Bian winning the election.
首次政黨輪替陳水扁勝選

2004
Chen Shui-Bian re-elected.
陳水扁連任

2008
Political party alternated again, with Ma Ying-Jeou winning the election.
政黨輪替馬英九勝選

After the Democratic Progressive Party (DPP) government came to power in the early 2000s, it released policy messages expressing a desire to open up tourism for mainland Chinese visitors to Taiwan. However, the Beijing government remained unresponsive to this message. It wasn't until 2005, when Lien Chan, representing the Kuomintang(KMT), visits China. On the basis of acknowledging the 1992 Consensus, established a platform for KMT-CCP cooperation.

In 2008, following the second change in ruling parties in Taiwan, Beijing officially began to open up tourism for mainland Chinese visitors to Taiwan. The message conveyed to the public was that they needed to support this pro-China and unification-friendly stance to benefit from economic incentives. From then, the number of Chinese tourists visiting Taiwan steadily increased, significantly impacting Taiwan's tourism industry and creating a "trade dependency relationship" between the tourism sectors of the two sides of the Taiwan Strait.

Due to this tourism trade dependency on China, in 2009, when the Kaohsiung Film Festival planned to screen the documentary "The Ten Conditions of Love" about Rebiya Kadeer, the spiritual leader of the Uyghur movement, tourism operators in Kaohsiung protested. However, these Taiwanese tourism operators may have played the role of "local collaborators," helping Beijing exert its policy and political influence.

In 2016, with Tsai Ing-wen becoming president. At this time, some tourism operators publicly urged Tsai Ing-wen to accept the 1992 Consensus. Beijing, in turn, stated that since Tsai Ing-wen did not endorse the 1992 Consensus, leading to a decline in mainland Chinese tourists visiting Taiwan.

2019
China suspended self-guided tours to Taiwan.
中國暫停陸客自由行

2012
Ma Ying-Jeou re-elected.
馬英九連任

2016
Political party alternated and Tsai Ing-Wen won the election.
政黨輪替蔡英文勝選

2020
Tsai Ing-Wen re-elected.
蔡英文連任

2024
Lai Ching-Te elected.
賴清德勝選

Source 資料來源（3）

China uses Taiwan's trade dependency on China's tourism industry as economic leverage, cultivating local collaborators to apply pressure. This strategy aims to apply pressure and influence the policy direction of the Taiwanese government, making this indirect reinforcement to Taiwan.

民進黨政府在 2000 年代初期上台後，曾規劃開放陸客來台觀光的政策，但北京政府對此訊息始終相應不理，一直到了 2005 年連戰代表國民黨訪中，承認九二共識，開啟國共合作平台。

2008 年台灣二次政黨輪替，北京正式開放陸客來台。這對台灣人民釋放出來的訊息是「親中，才有糖吃」。從這一年開始，陸客來台人數持續上升，對台灣的旅遊觀光業帶來很大的影響，因此產生了兩岸之間觀光業的「貿易依賴關係」。

因為台灣旅遊業對中國的貿易依賴，在 2009 年的高雄電影節，原先計畫播放維吾爾精神領袖熱比婭的紀錄片《愛的十個條件》，受到高雄旅遊業者出面抗議。這些台灣的旅遊業者，就屬於「在地協力者」，協助北京來對台發揮影響力。

2016 年蔡英文總統上台，這時，我們可以看到有旅遊業者出面呼籲蔡英文接受九二共識，而北京則出面表示，蔡英文沒有完成九二共識的答卷，因此陸客就不來了。台灣觀光旅遊業對中國遊客的貿易依賴，就是中國的經濟槓桿，培養在地協力者，希望藉此施加壓力，影響台灣的政策走向。

Investment dependency and local collaboration: Taiwanese business investments
投資依賴與在地協力：台商投資

During the 2012 Taiwan's presidential election, 19 Taiwanese businesspeople collectively stood up to support the 1992 Consensus, urging the Taiwanese public to support the Consensus and the parties that endorsed it.
These 19 businesspeople were members of the Cross-strait political and business network, having participated in the Cross-Strait Entrepreneurs Summit in China. These businesspeople, due to their investments in China, whether acting voluntarily or being mobilized, had to align with Beijing's policies. This is also evidence of Taiwan's dependence on investment as part of China's influence.

2012 年台灣總統大選，有 19 位台商不約而同站出來支持九二共識，並呼籲台灣民眾支持認同九二共識的政黨。

這 19 位台商，是跨海峽政商網絡的成員之一，甚至參與了中國的兩岸企業家峰會。這些台商可能因為在中國的投資，無論出於自發性或是被動員，都必須呼應北京的政策，這也是投資依賴作為中國對台影響力的事證之一。

On the case of Taiwanese businesspeople, did this mobilization around the 1992 Consensus actually have a significant impact on the election results? According to the research by Wu Jiemin and Liao Mei, the answer is affirmative. In the paper, two statistical models were compared.

From the above two cases, we can see that China often uses Taiwan's economic dependence on China to mobilize local collaborators in Taiwan to respond to Beijing's political needs, aiming to influence Taiwan's political outcomes.

在台商的案例中,這種對九二共識的議題動員,事實上真的有對選舉結果造成影響嗎?以吳介民跟廖美的研究來看,答案是肯定的。

透過陸客觀光與在中台商兩個案例,中國時常藉由台灣對中國的經濟依賴,動員台灣在地的協力者,呼應北京的政治需求,企圖達到影響台灣政治的結果。

1-3 China's influence revealed: China's propaganda and disinformation operations in Taiwan
影響力現形：媒體宣傳背後的中國銳實力

Influence operation model: sharp power operating model for global geopolitics

影響力運作模式：全球地緣政治脈絡－銳實力運作模式

proving the existence of China's influence, we need to understand the sharp power operational mode that authoritarian states are most incentivized to employ.

證明中國影響力確實存在後，我們要來認識威權國家最有誘因去使用的銳實力運作模式。

Hard power
硬實力

Sharp power
銳實力

Soft power
軟實力

Sharp Power 銳實力：

- It can be understood as a "special form of hard power," appearing as soft power on the surface, but it is actually hard power behind it.

- Mainly through covert, penetrative coercion and inducement means, it attempt to achieve the aims of "soft power," which aims to change the internal perceptions of the target.

- 可以理解成為「特殊形態的硬實力」，外表看起來是軟實力，背後卻是硬實力

- 主要透過隱蔽性、滲透性的強制跟誘因的手段，來嘗試著達到「軟實力」希望達到的、改變對方內在認知的目標

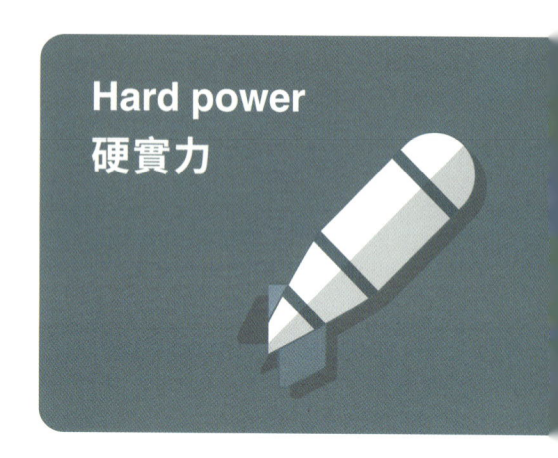

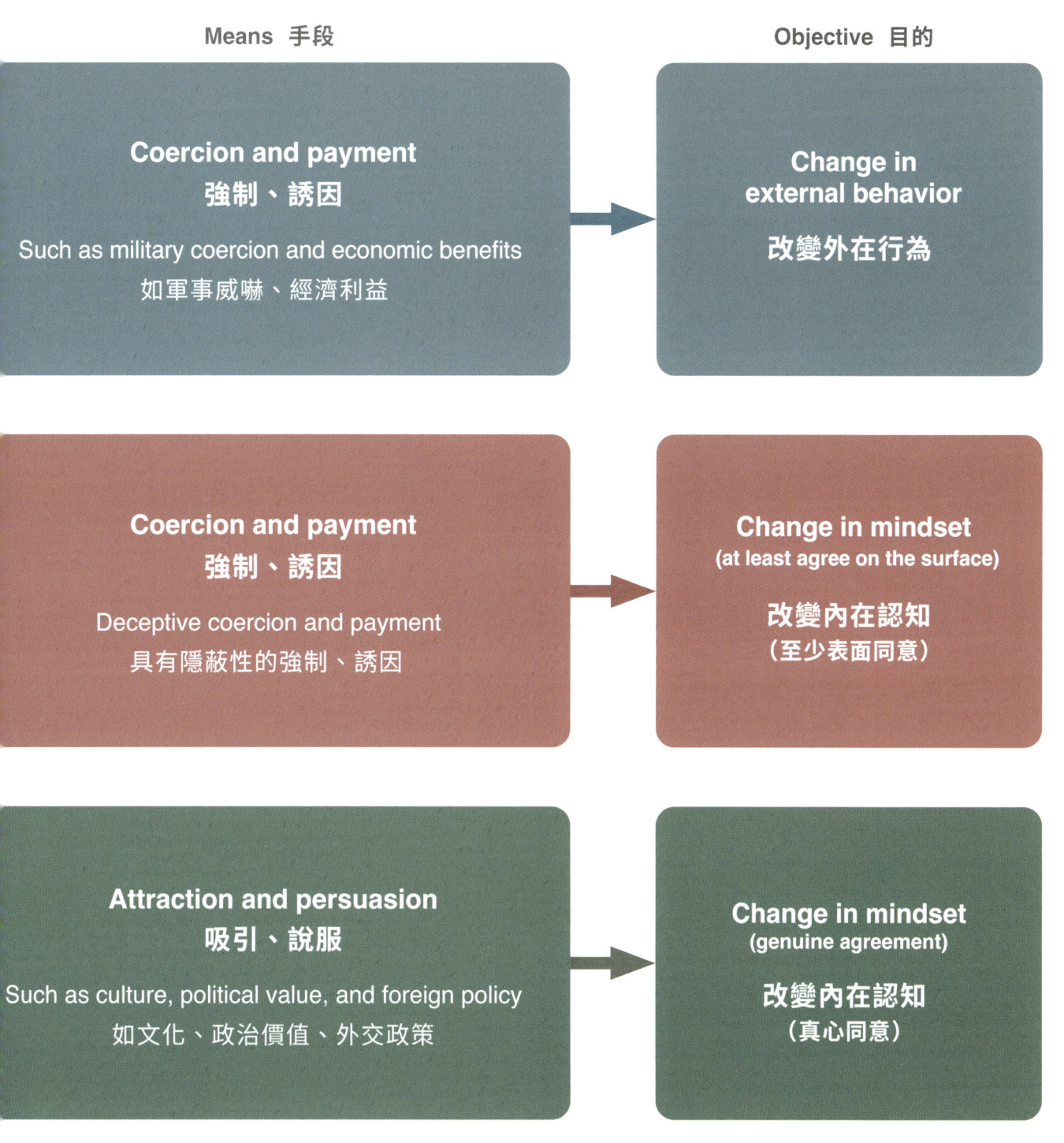

Means 手段		Objective 目的
Coercion and payment 強制、誘因 Such as military coercion and economic benefits 如軍事威嚇、經濟利益	→	**Change in external behavior** 改變外在行為
Coercion and payment 強制、誘因 Deceptive coercion and payment 具有隱蔽性的強制、誘因	→	**Change in mindset** (at least agree on the surface) 改變內在認知 （至少表面同意）
Attraction and persuasion 吸引、說服 Such as culture, political value, and foreign policy 如文化、政治價值、外交政策	→	**Change in mindset** (genuine agreement) 改變內在認知 （真心同意）

Source 資料來源（4）

The operational model of sharp power
銳實力運作模式

The operational model of sharp power primarily involves three characteristics:

而銳實力的運作模式，主要有三個特徵：

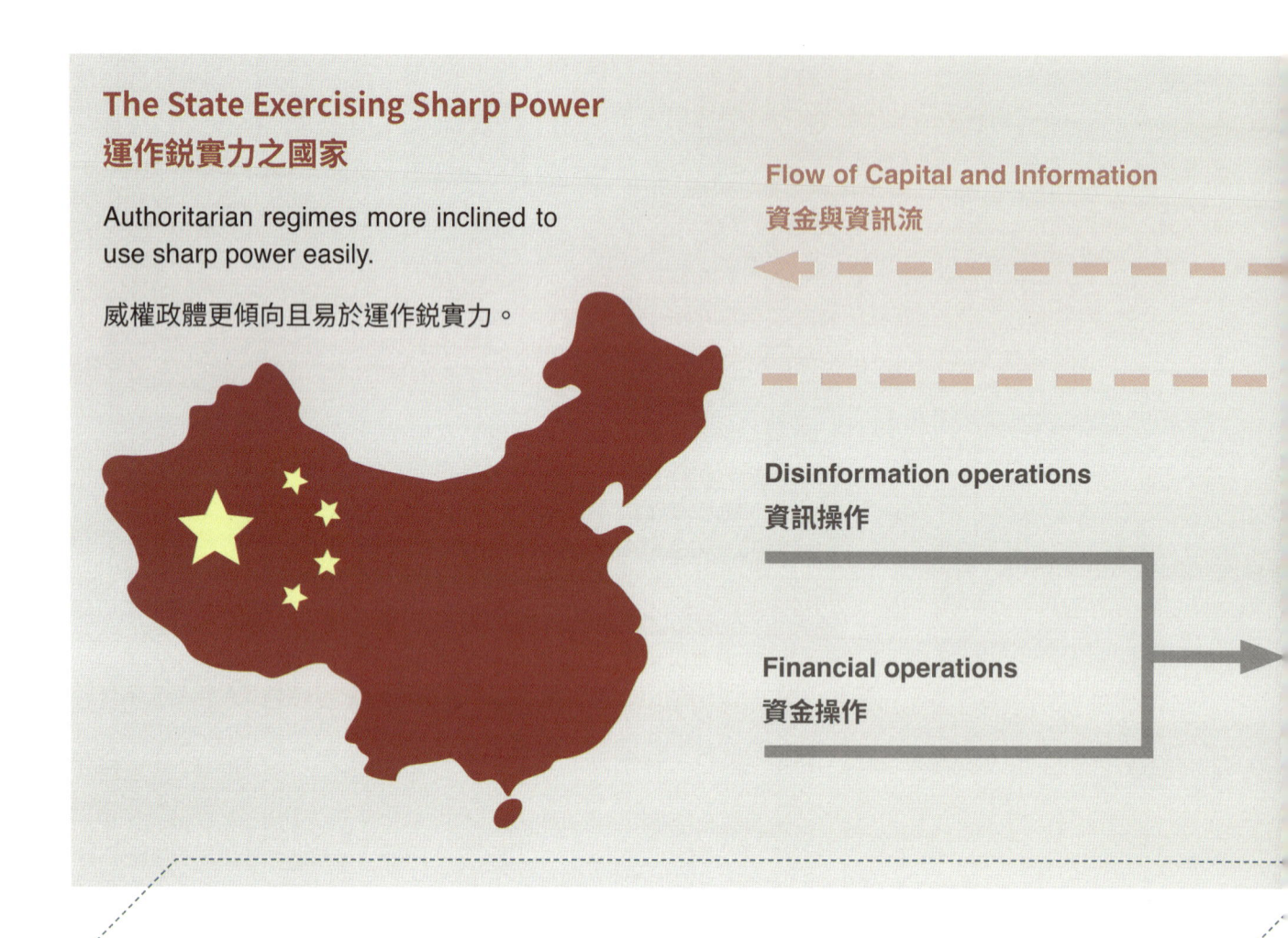

Step 1 Background 背景 ▸ **Step 2** Means 手段 ▸ **Step 3** Aims 目標

The State Exercising Sharp Power
運作銳實力之國家

Authoritarian regimes more inclined to use sharp power easily.

威權政體更傾向且易於運作銳實力。

Flow of Capital and Information
資金與資訊流

Disinformation operations
資訊操作

Financial operations
資金操作

No internal democratic oversight mechanism to limit operational tactics.

無內部民主監督機制去限制手段。

For example 舉例

- Create false information or conspiracy theories; and use Taiwan's Internet freedom to influence Taiwan's media and public opinion.
- Use capital to mobilize Taiwanese local collaborators; assist with, create, or spread false information or biased information.
- Use information to mobilize "non-specific local collaborators."
- 製造假訊息或陰謀論，利用台灣網路自由，影響台灣媒體與輿論。
- 透過資金動員台灣在地協力者，協助、產製或傳播假訊息或是偏差的資訊。
- 透過資訊操作動員「非特定的在地協力者」。

Step 1 — Background 背景

Create asymmetrical exchanges of capital and information.
創造資金與資訊的不對稱交流。

Content censorship and selective disclosure used to achieve asymmetrical exchange.
透過內容審查、選擇性開放達成不對稱交流。

For example 舉例

Use film and television censorship and the Great Firewall to censor external information.
透過影視審查與網路長城，讓外界資訊不易進入。

Taiwan is a country bombarded with disinformation, but China is not.
臺灣是嚴重受到假消息攻擊的國家，但中國不是。

Targeted Country: Taiwan
目標國家：臺灣

Step 2 — Means 手段

Deceptive Operation of Coercion & Payment.
隱蔽性的強制與誘因。

Step 3 — Aims 目標

Promoting Authoritarianism / Discrediting Democracy
貶抑民主 / 拉抬威權

Source 資料來源（5）

Lack democratic legitimacy; need to create advantages in influence.
缺乏民主正當性，更需要創造影響力優勢。

Cases that affect Taiwan 對台影響案例

- Etrimental to the democratic communication or democratic consensus.
- Influencing voters' decision and election results.
- Impacting the confidence Taiwanese people have towards democracy.
- 不利民主溝通、民主共識之形成。
- 影響選民投票意向，進而影響選舉結果。
- 衝擊台灣民眾對民主的信心。

Next, we will analyze the sharp power of China behind the Taiwanese media propaganda arena.

接下來，我們就要來觀察台灣媒體宣傳場域背後的中國銳實力。

China's sharp power means: media propaganda
中國銳實力手段：媒體宣傳

Firstly, let's review significant events in Taiwan's media landscape over the past decade:
On the left side of the timeline, we see various incidents illustrating China's influence on Taiwanese media across different dimensions. On the right side, we observe the responses from the Taiwanese government and society to this series of influences exerted by China in the media sphere. Such as the "Anti-Media Monopoly Movement" starting in 2012, and the Sunflower Movement in 2014. This response included actions from the Control Yuan and the National Communications Commission (NCC), which began addressing related issues.

首先，我們回顧過去的台灣媒體界，有哪些重要事件：
時間軸的左邊，是中國對台灣媒體的影響力運作事件；時間軸的右邊，則是台灣政府與社會的反制與回應。如 2012 年的反媒體壟斷運動、2014 年的太陽花運動，以及監察院與 NCC 對媒體壟斷與服貿協定的回應。

China's influence events towards Taiwan
中國對台影響事件

2008
Tsai Eng-meng acquired China Times, China Television Company, and CTI Television Incorporation.
蔡衍明收購中時、中視、中天

2009
The first Cross-strait Media Summit was held.
跨海峽媒體峰會首次舉辦

2012
A media placement incident of Fujian province governor's visit to Taiwan. SET canceled its political commentary program "Da Hua Xin Wen" (Big Talk News)
福建省長來台置入行銷事件
三立停播大話新聞

2015
Cher Wang invested in TVBS
The first Cross-Strait Media Summit in Beijing was held.
王雪紅入股 TVBS
兩岸媒體人北京峰會首次舉辦

2018
The Kansai Airport fake news incident.
關西機場假新聞事件

Source 資料來源（6） 這裡提供的範例具時效性內容

Event of Taiwan's resistance to disinformation from China
台灣反作用力事件

2010
The Control Yuan proposed corrective action for China's media placement incident.
監察院就中國置入行銷提糾正案

2012
Anti-ChinaTimes Movement and Anti-Media Monopoly Movement.
拒絕中時運動、反媒體壟斷運動

2013
NCC rejected the Want Want-CNS merger.
NCC 決議旺中併購中嘉案不予通過

2014
The Sunflower Student Movement
318 運動

2019
The Anti-Red Media Movement
NCC started to penalize television channels for failure to conduct fact-checking
反紅媒運動
NCC 開始開罰電視臺違反事實查證

2020
NCC decided not to renew Cti News' license.
NCC 決議中天新聞不予換照

According to this diagram, China's influence on Taiwanese media primarily involves indirect financial manipulation, which is a part of the operation mode of sharp power. The Chinese government first creates an asymmetrical financial exchange situation between China and Taiwan and then utilizes three major channels: the ownership market, the advertising market, and the circulation market. Through financial influence, they mobilize specific local collaborators in Taiwan to achieve their political objectives.

中國對台灣媒體的影響，是屬於間接影響中的資金操作，這也是銳實力運作模式的一部分。中國政府，首先透過營造中國與台灣資金的不對稱交流情況，然後經由三個重要管道：所有權市場、廣告市場以及發行市場，透過資金影響，動員特定的在地協力者，在台灣遂行他的政治目的。

```
Chinese government 中國政府
├── Direct influence 直接影響
└── Indirect influence 間接影響
    ├── Financial operations 資金操作
    │   ├── Ownership market 所有權市場
    │   ├── Advertising market 廣告市場
    │   └── Circulation market 發行市場
    └── Disinformation operations 資訊操作
```

Specific local collaborators 特定在地協力者

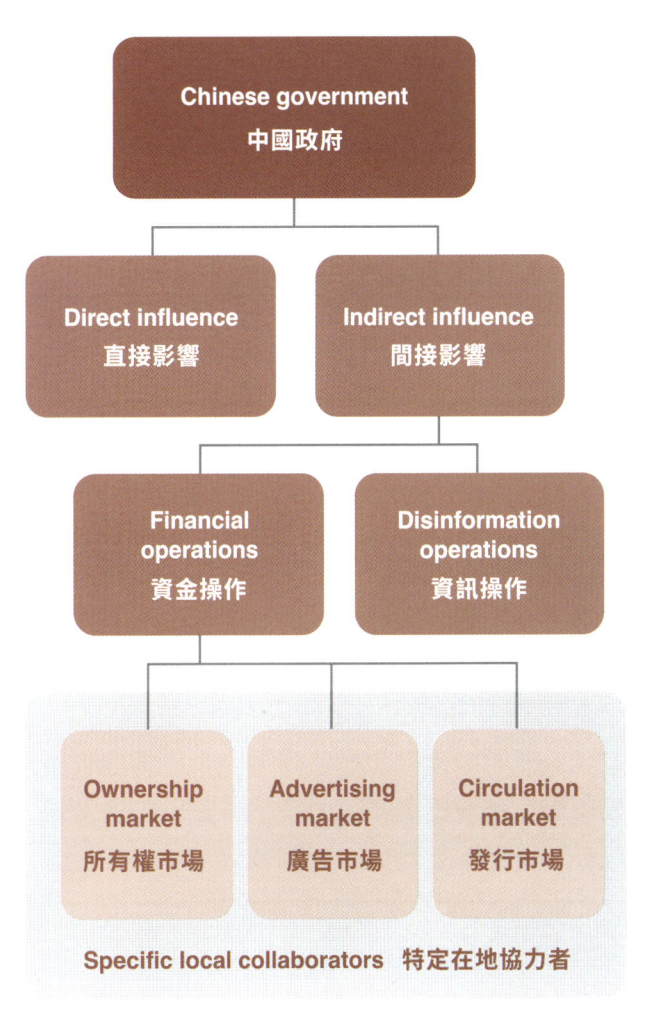

Source 資料來源（7）

21

Ownership market
所有權市場

Taiwan does not allow Chinese capital to invest in its media industry. However, Beijing can still penetrate the Taiwanese media through financial exchanges with pro-China Taiwanese businesspeople. The most classic example of this is the Want Want China Times Group.

From the data compiled from the financial reports of China's Want Want Group, it shows that Want Want received financial subsidies from the Chinese government as early as 2008. After Tsai Eng-meng acquired Taiwan's China Times, CTV, and CTiTV and established the Want Want China Times Media Group, the subsidies received by Want Want from the Chinese government doubled in 2009.

It is important to note that the financial subsidies from China to the Want Want Group were not directly provided to the Want Want China Times Media Group in Taiwan but rather to the subsidiary of Want Want Group in mainland China.

Thus, we can see that the Want Want Group has a substantial economic and financial dependency on the Chinese government. This dependency creates leverage in the ownership market, allowing Beijing to infiltrate Taiwanese media and exert its political influence.

台灣政府並不允許中資投資台灣的媒體產業，可是北京仍然可以藉由與親中台商之間的資金往來，滲透台灣媒體，其中最經典的案例就是旺中集團。

從中國旺旺的財報數據來看，中國旺旺在2008年就接受中國政府的資金補貼，而在蔡衍明陸續收購了台灣的中時、中視跟中天，成立了旺旺中時媒體集團之後，中國旺旺在2009年，從中國政府拿到的補貼是直接翻倍。

中國對旺旺集團的資金補貼，並不是直接提供給在台灣的旺旺中時媒體集團，而是提供給旺旺集團在中國大陸的子公司。

因此，旺中集團對於中國政府，具有實質的經濟依賴跟財務依賴，這便構成了在所有權市場裡頭的槓桿，讓北京可以滲透台灣的媒體，藉此施加他的政治影響。

The amount of subsidies that Want Want China Holdings Ltd. received from the Chinese government (in thousand US dollars)

中國旺旺收受中國政府補助金額（千美元）

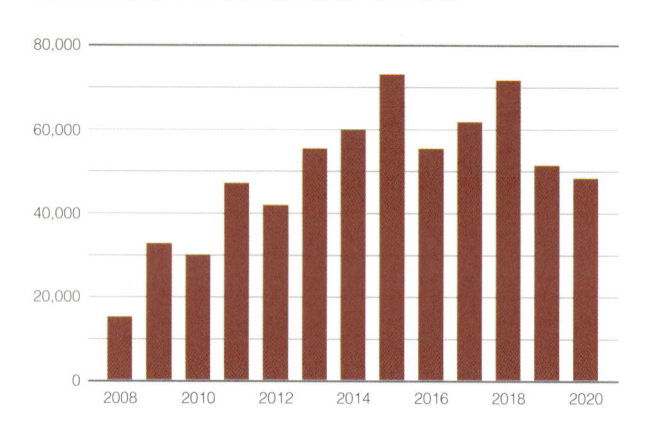

The proportion of Chinese government subsidies in Want Want China Holdings' revenue.

中國旺旺收受中國政府補助佔利潤之比例

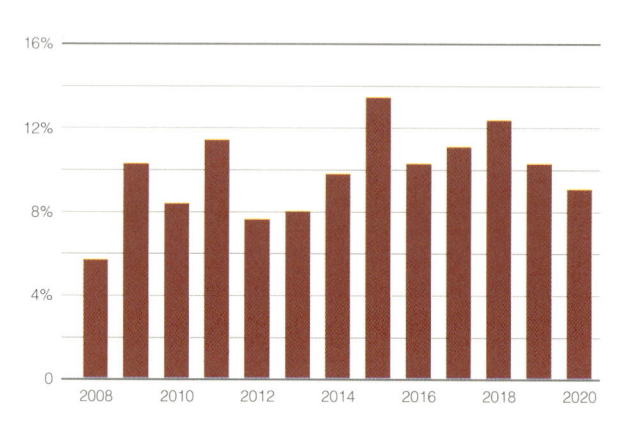

Source 資料來源（8）
註：引用黃兆年的研究

Advertising market
廣告市場

Despite the regulations in the Cross-Strait Act stating that Taiwanese media cannot publish advertisements from China without permission from Taiwanese authorities, there have been covert operations assisting China in placing advertorials. The Control Yuan has issued investigative reports highlighting that some Taiwanese media have illegally accepted advertorial funds from China's Taiwan Affairs Office or provincial and city governments to publish news reports or special features promoting China politically.

One notable example is a 2012 news report by Newtalk, which revealed that the Want Want China Times Group, during the visit of the Governor of Fujian Province to Taiwan in 2012, collaborated with the Fujian Provincial Government and Xiamen Municipal Government on an advertorial plan. The table on the right clearly shows the scheduled exposure dates, pages, themes, and content, representing a concrete case of advertorial placement.

Additionally, around 2020, Reuters conducted an investigative report indicating that at least five other media outlets were continuously engaged in illegal native advertising for China.

雖然兩岸關係條例中規範，在台灣當局未許可的情況下，媒體並不能夠刊登來自中國的廣告，但實務上，一直有媒體協助中國刊登置入性行銷廣告。監察院曾有調查報告指出，一些台灣媒體違法收受來自中國國台辦或是省市政府所提供的置入性行銷經費，刊登新聞報導或專題去為中國做政治宣傳。

2012 年新頭殼的新聞報導就曾揭露，2012 年福建省長訪台期間，旺中集團配合福建省政府跟廈門市政府的置入性行銷計劃。在計劃表裡，對廣告曝光的日期、版面、主題跟內容都有規範，是非常具體的置入性行銷案例。

另外，在 2020 年前後，路透社也有調查報導指出，台灣至少還有五家媒體，持續的在做違法的置入性行銷廣告。

"Meeting with Lien Chan, Su Shulin says Pingtan is a great gift for Lien"
ChinaTimes 2012/03/28
〈會連戰 蘇樹林稱平潭是大禮〉
中時新聞網 2012/03/28

Source 資料來源（9）

Circulation markets
發行市場

Apart from the ownership and advertising markets, the distribution market is another critical channel through which Beijing influences Taiwanese media through financial means.

A case to discuss is the efforts of Sanlih E-Television (SET) from the late 2000s to the mid-2010s to enter the Chinese market, achieving some success. In 2011, SET executives announced the "Huaju" project, promoting dramas to the Chinese market under the term "Huaju" (Chinese dramas) instead of "Taiju" (Taiwanese dramas), to align with Beijing's preferences. During this process, SET canceled its flagship political commentary program "Da Hua Xin Wen" (Big Talk News) in 2012, which some believe was a direct or indirect result of hints from China's State Administration of Radio, Film, and Television.

However, by the mid-2010s, the export of idol dramas faced bottlenecks, possibly because Chinese authorities deemed SET TV's content overly Taiwan-centric, or due to rising protectionism in China's film and television industry. By 2014-2015, SET found it challenging to expand in the Chinese market. As a result, in 2017, Zheng Hongyi, the former host of the canceled "Big Talk News," was brought back to host other programs on SET.

除了所有權市場、廣告市場之外，發行市場也是北京透過資金影響台灣媒體的重要管道。

我們以比較偏本土派的三立電視台為例。三立電視台從 2000 年代末期，一直到 2010 年代中葉以前，都嘗試進軍中國市場，甚至在 2011 年時，電視台高層宣布了「華劇」的計劃，將要推廣至中國市場的戲劇稱為「華劇」而非「台劇」，藉此迎合北京官方。而在這個過程裡，三立電視台在 2012 年時，停播了招牌政論節目「大話新聞」，有人認為這是直接或間接的受到中國廣電總局的暗示。

但是到了 2010 年代中期，三立的偶像劇出口中國計劃遇到了瓶頸，可能是中國官方認為三立的台灣意識色彩仍太重，也可能是中國 2010 年代中期的影視產業保護主義興起。總之 2014 年後，三立已經很難在中國市場有所拓展。因此，在 2017 年時，停播的「大話新聞」的主持人鄭弘儀，又被找回三立電視台主持節目了。

Export of SET's TV shows to China
三立電視劇輸出中國市場播出情形

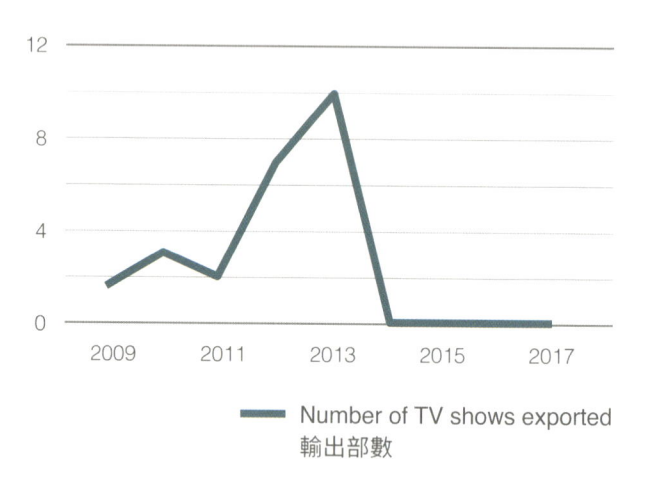

— Number of TV shows exported
輸出部數

2011, Sanlih E-Television
The first of the SET prime time drama "Inborn Pair"
2011 年 三立電視台
華人電視劇八點檔系列首部作品〈真愛找麻煩〉

Source 資料來源 (10)
註：引用黃兆年的研究

Media's self-censorship
媒體自我審查

Lastly, we will have to discuss the impact of China's financial manipulation and leverage in the ownership, advertising, and distribution markets on Taiwanese media, leading to media "self-censorship".The financial manipulation and leverage by China in Taiwanese media ownership, advertising market, and distribution market have led to self-censorship within the media, causing significant harm to freedom of speech.

The left case involves the China Times' reporting frequency on the sensitive topics of the Tiananmen Square incident and the Dalai Lama. Before and after 2009, the reporting ratio was about 5 to 1, indicating that the China Times reported more extensively on these sensitive issues before being acquired by pro-China businesspeople. However, after 2009, the reporting significantly decreased.

中國對台灣媒體的所有權市場、廣告市場與發行市場的資金操作與槓桿，造成媒體內部自我審查，對言論自由造成很大的傷害。

我們來看中國時報對六四與西藏達賴喇嘛這兩個敏感話題的報導數量統計。以 2009 年為界，比例大約是 5 比 1。也就是說，中國時報在被親中台商收購前，會用大篇幅來報導中國的敏感議題，可是 2009 年之後，報導比例就很明顯的下降。

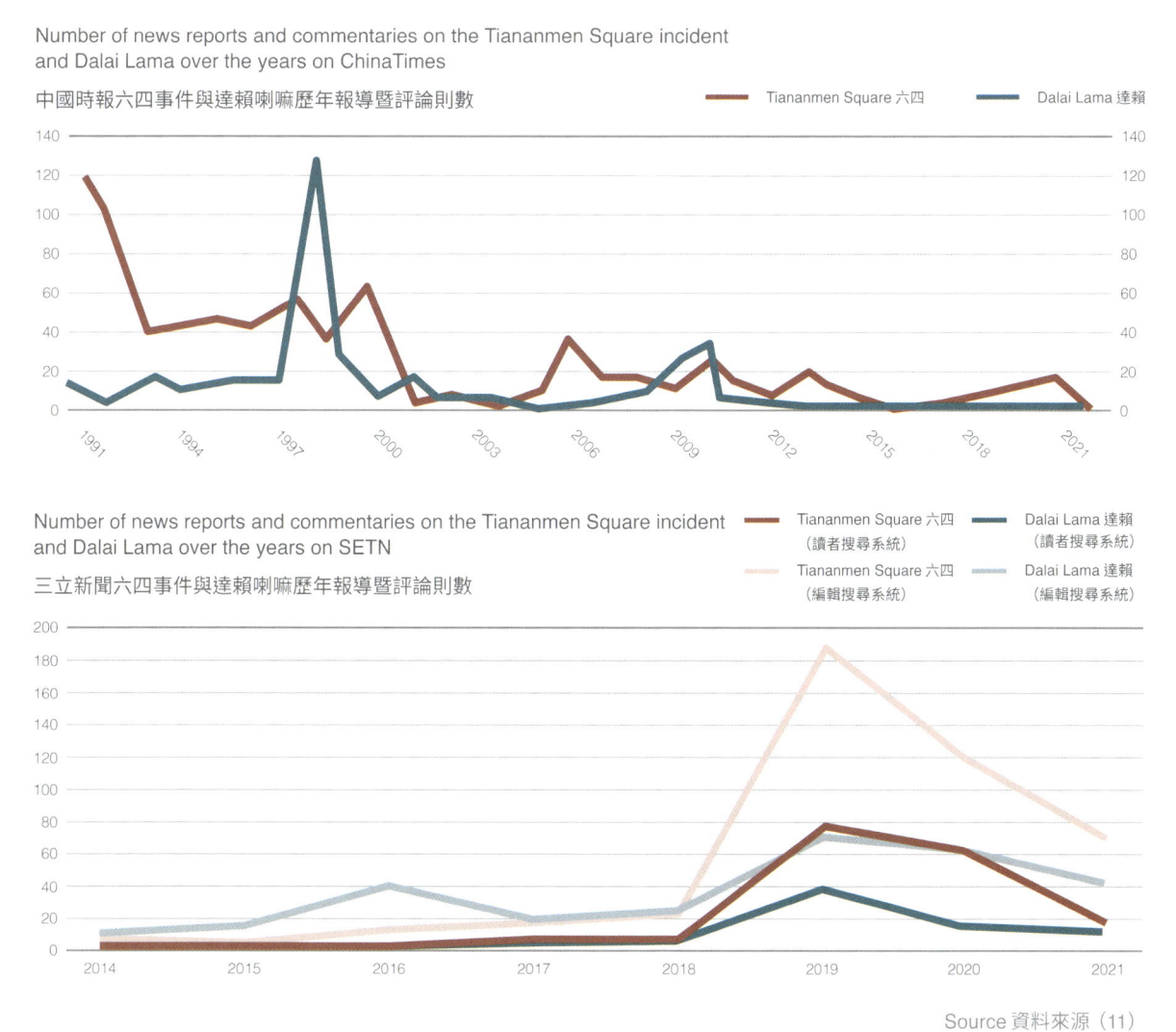

Number of news reports and commentaries on the Tiananmen Square incident and Dalai Lama over the years on ChinaTimes
中國時報六四事件與達賴喇嘛歷年報導暨評論則數

Number of news reports and commentaries on the Tiananmen Square incident and Dalai Lama over the years on SETN
三立新聞六四事件與達賴喇嘛歷年報導暨評論則數

Source 資料來源（11）

1-4
Signal flares in the fog: information manipulation and information literacy
迷霧裡的信號彈：資訊操弄與資訊判讀

Methods and objectives of CCP's information manipulation against Taiwan
中國對台資訊操弄的手法與目標

What are the methods of China's information manipulation against Taiwan?
Many might think that only information directly initiated by China qualifies as CCP's information manipulation against Taiwan. However, past research and collected data show that not only official Chinese entities (like the Taiwan Affairs Office or China's Ministry of Foreign Affairs) and state media (such as Global Times or People's Daily) engage in information manipulation against Taiwan. It can also be done through collaborative dissemination groups that amplify these narratives. This

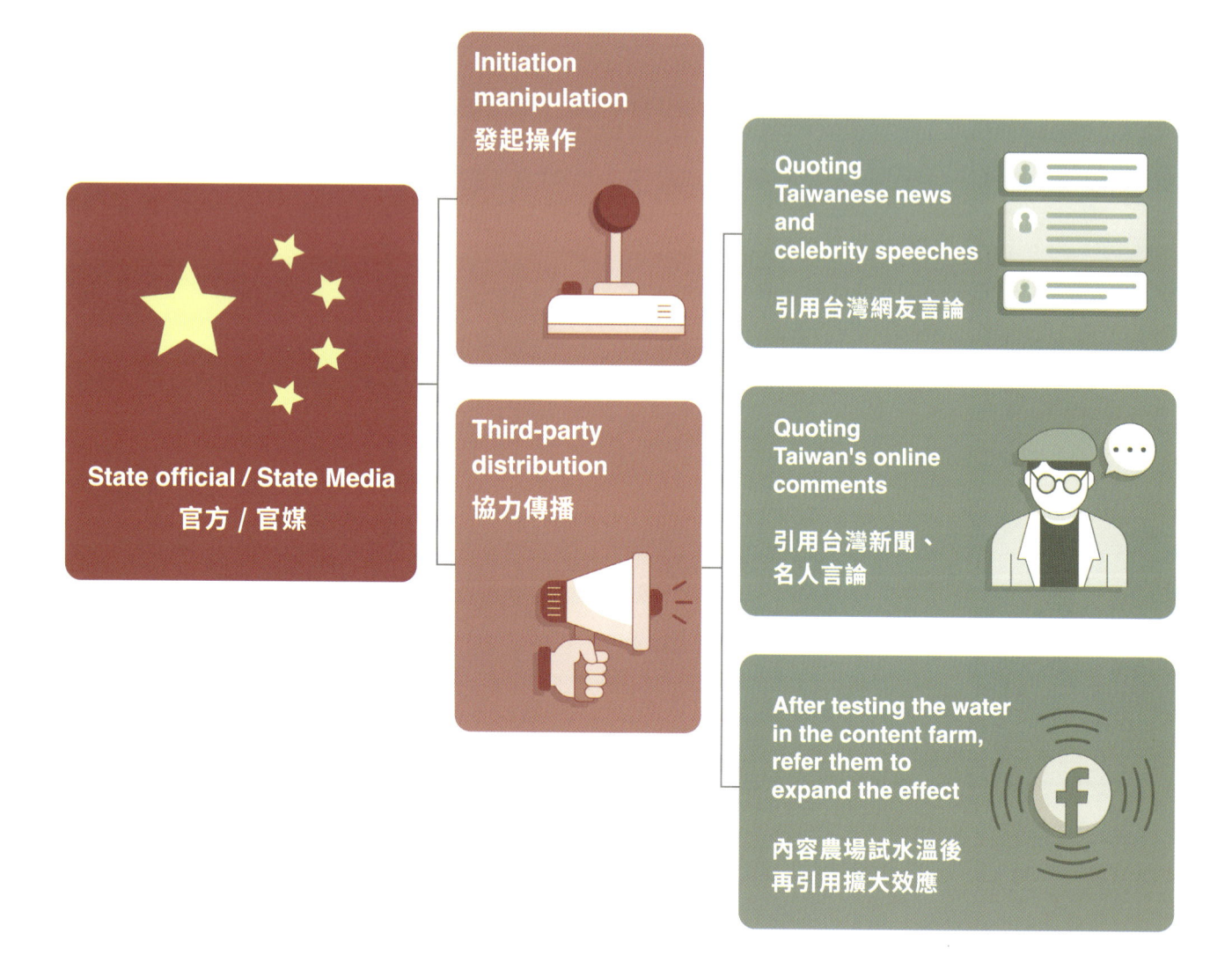

State official / State Media
官方 / 官媒

- **Initiation manipulation** 發起操作
- **Third-party distribution** 協力傳播
  - **Quoting Taiwanese news and celebrity speeches** 引用台灣網友言論
  - **Quoting Taiwan's online comments** 引用台灣新聞、名人言論
  - **After testing the water in the content farm, refer them to expand the effect** 內容農場試水溫後再引用擴大效應

includes citing relevant Taiwanese news, political commentary shows, and pundits, a method we call "using Taiwan against Taiwan."

The purpose of this information manipulation, we believe, is for China to create a worldview that aligns with CCP interests. This involves two aspects: first, discrediting Taiwan's democratic system and governance, making democracy appear unfeasible; second, undermining Taiwan's democratic alliances, including spreading skepticism towards the U.S. and Japan, known as "doubting America" and "doubting Japan" narratives.

中國對台的資訊操弄，會用哪些手法呢？

很多人會覺得，只有由中國發起的，才叫做中共對台資訊操弄。但在過去的研究以及資料顯示，不僅僅只有中國官方（如國台辦、中國外交部）、官媒（如環球日報、人民日報）會對台灣發起資訊操弄，中國也會經由台灣在地協力團體，進一步傳播、放大這些言論的影響力。這其中包含引用台灣的新聞、政論節目名嘴等等，我們稱之為以台制台。

中國資訊操弄的目的，是在創造符合中共利益的世界觀。這包含兩個層面，第一個是否定台灣的民主制度以及治理，讓民主變得不可行；第二個則是去破壞台灣的民主同盟關係，包含針對美國跟日本的疑美論和疑日論等。

To create a worldview that is aligned with CCP's benefits
創造符合中共利益的世界觀

Negate the democratic system and administration
否定民主制度及治理
- Democratic deficit ● 民主無用
- Corruption ● 貪污
- Ballot stuffing ● 作票
- …… ● ……

Negate the Democratic League
否定民主同盟
- America Skepticism ● 疑美論
- Japan Skepticism ● 疑日論
- …… ● ……

Source 資料來源（12）

Information credibility evaluation
訊息可信度評量

How can we determine the authenticity and reliability of information in the face of China's information manipulation? For "discourse-based information manipulation," we can use the four-step "information credibility evaluation." This involves evaluating the content, source, and inference aspects of the information to identify suspicious messages, and finally making a comprehensive judgment on the likelihood of the information.

Next, let's explain each step in detail.
First is step one, deconstructing the message, distinguishing between facts and opinions. A "factual statement" includes two definitions: first, that something has already happened, and second, that it can be verified as true or false. Statements that meet these two definitions can be called "factual statements."

An opinion, on the other hand, is a view or belief that may or may not be based on facts. If an opinion lacks a factual basis, then its credibility is not worth discussing.

The second step is to verify the facts and content sources. This includes whether the source is correct and professional, and whether it can be verified. Regarding content, attention should be paid to whether it includes altered or incorrect information.

In this step, the most important thing is to verify if there is a secondary source for the information. If the information is true, it will definitely not be exclusive to a single news outlet or only exist on some content farm websites. Therefore, we should develop an awareness of the importance of secondary sources. We can use fact-checking centers or websites like "Cofacts" to perform thorough verification from multiple sources.

The third step is to examine whether the inference is reasonable.
Common issues in the inference process include generalizing from a limited scope and false analogies. For example, in many event reports,

Step 1 | Dissect message → Distinguish facts from viewpoints
拆解訊息 → 區分事實與觀點

→

Step 2 | Audit the factual 'source' and 'contents.'
查核事實「來源」及「內容」

→

you often see the media quoting "netizens' opinions." However, the views of some netizens cannot represent the entire opinion. Therefore, we must be more careful in examining whether the inference process of the information is reasonable.

Finally, of course, we need to compile the suspicious or non-suspicious aspects we found in the above steps and make a comprehensive judgment on the credibility of the message.

面對中國的資訊操弄,我們該如何判斷訊息的真實性與可信度呢?我們可以透過「訊息可信度評量」的四步驟,分別針對內容、來源、推論三個面向,最後綜合判斷此訊息的是否為真。

接下來,我們要更仔細說明各個步驟的內容。
首先是步驟一,拆解訊息,區分出事實和觀點。「事實陳述」包含了兩個定義,第一,這件事情已經發生,第二,這件事情可以被驗證是正確或錯誤,符合這兩個定義的陳述就可以稱為「事實陳述」。
而觀點則是一種看法跟意見,觀點需要事實基礎作為根據,如果沒有,我們就不太需要去討論它的可信度。

接著是第二步,查核事實來源及內容。事實的來源是否正確、專業,是否可以被驗證;而在查核內容時,則要注意是否為變造的內容,或錯誤內容等。
在這個步驟,最重要的事情是查核這個訊息是否有第二來源。如果這個訊息為真,它絕對不會只有某一間新聞的獨家,或是只存在於某個內容農場網站,所以我們應該要培養對第二消息來源的重視,而這部份,我們可以透過事實查核中心,或者是「Cofacts 真的假的」這樣的訊息查核網站,來做多方的驗證。

第三步驟,檢驗推論是否合理。
在推論過程中常見的問題,包含以偏概全、錯誤類比等。例如,在許多新聞報導當中,常常會看到記者引用「網友說」。但部分網友的意見或觀點,並不能用來概稱全體的觀點,所以我們必須更小心地看待資訊的推論過程是否合理。

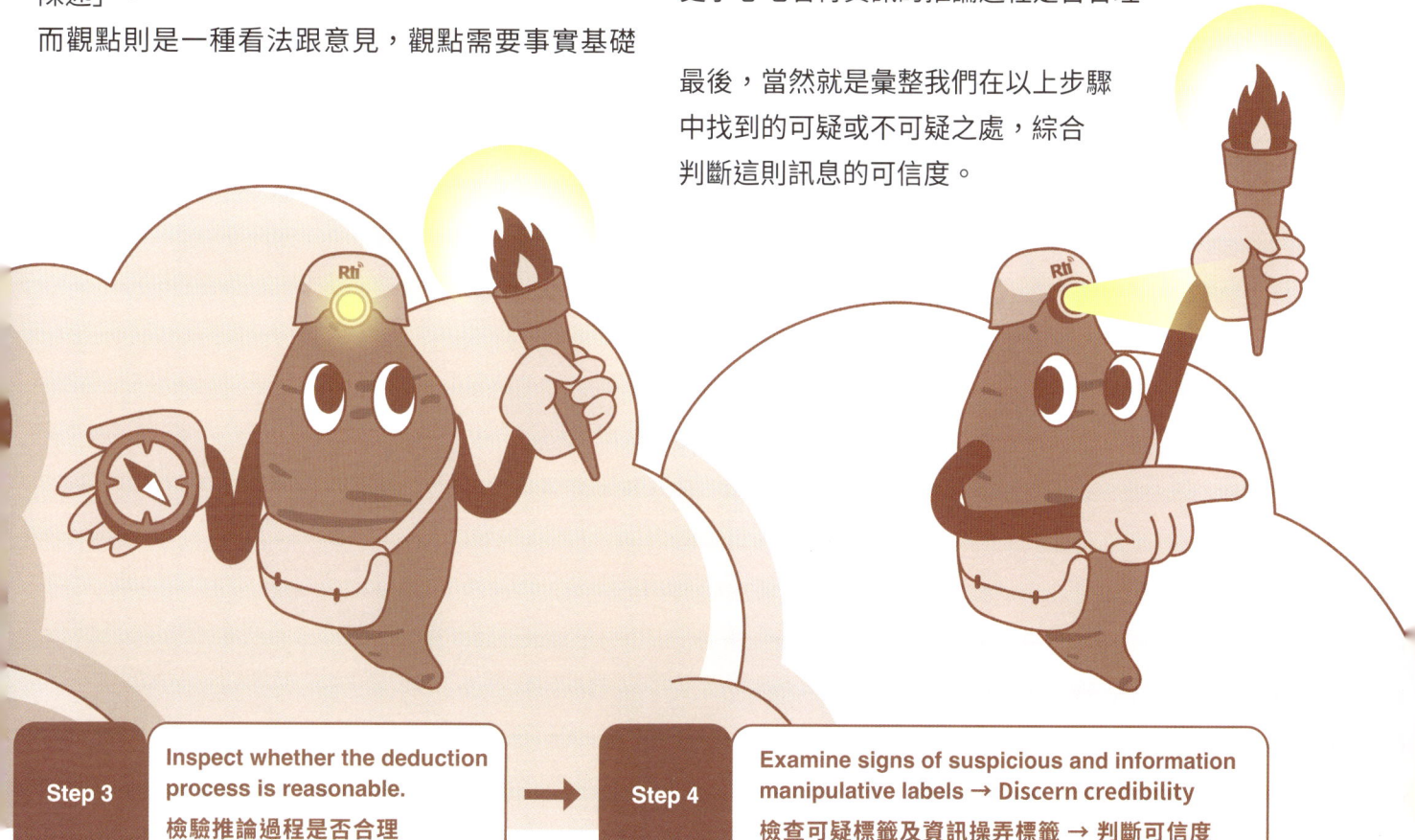

最後,當然就是彙整我們在以上步驟中找到的可疑或不可疑之處,綜合判斷這則訊息的可信度。

| Step 3 | Inspect whether the deduction process is reasonable. 檢驗推論過程是否合理 | → | Step 4 | Examine signs of suspicious and information manipulative labels → Discern credibility 檢查可疑標籤及資訊操弄標籤 → 判斷可信度 |

1-5
Out of the foggy battlefield: case studies of China's information manipulation against Taiwan
走出迷霧戰場：中國對臺資訊操弄案例

Let's look at three very clear examples to illustrate how China conducts information manipulation against Taiwan.

我們要用三個例子，來跟大家說明中國對台資訊操弄如何進行。

1

Visit by Nancy Pelosi to Taiwan
裴洛西來台

- The information manipulation has been on one of the largest scales on the highest level in recent years, a fact publicly acknowledged by CCP's state media publicly.

- Versatile means: Apart from content directly originating from state media, some posts were made by hacked accounts and then quoted by state media to amplify their reach.

- 近年中共資訊操弄規模最大、層級最高，甚至中共官媒公開承認

- 手法多元，除直接官媒發起，另有盜帳號發文再以官媒引用擴大

2
TSMC's link to America skepticism
台積電與疑美論

- CCP state media's 'TikTok accounts' often works with Taiwanese public personalities to initiate the U.S.'s 'Say Goodbye to Taiwan' opinion.

- The phenomena and effect of content farm's mass posting.

- 中共官媒早於台灣名嘴一年,就已發起美國棄台論

- 內容農場群聚發文的現象及效果

3
Biological weapon
生物戰劑

- Evidence of the information manipulation initiated by the CCP government officially.
  Other examples include the COVID-19 origins hypothesis (Military World Games), and Zhao Lijian's misinterpretation of former U.S. President Jimmy Carter.

- 中共官方發起資訊操弄的實證
  其他例子包括 COVID 病毒起源論(軍運會)、趙立堅曲解卡特總統

Source 資料來源 (13)

Case one: visit by Nancy Pelosi to Taiwan
案例一：裴洛西訪台

In August 2022, Nancy Pelosi visited Taiwan, which sparked nine major discourse narratives of information manipulation. These nine narratives can be categorized into two types: the first type is directly initiated by the CCP, while the second type involves the use of hijacked accounts on social media platforms, which are then further disseminated by CCP state media to amplify their influence.

2022 年 8 月裴洛西來台，出現了這九大資訊操弄論述，而這九大內容，其實有兩種類型：第一種類型是由中共直接發起的，第二種類型則是透過盜用帳號於社交平台上發文，中共官媒再進一步去協力傳播，擴大它的影響力。

1 CCP: Su-35 jets were sent to The Taiwan Strait.
中共：蘇 35 戰機穿越台灣海峽

2 Fruit exporter Lui: Taiwan's fruit industry should target the mainland market; the government is harming exporters and farmers alike.
劉姓水果出口商：台灣水果一定要爭取大陸市場；政府害死出口商，農民也一定會受害

3 Using hacked PPT accounts to pose as pomelo farmers and falsely claimed: Pelosi's visit to Taiwan was an indication of negative impact on the chip industry, the election campaign, and could be a ploy for financial gain. They claimed the ban on pomelo exports to China, jeopardizing the livelihoods of families involved, leading to Taiwan losing the Taiwan Strait centerline and jeopardizing peace.
盜用 PTT 帳號冒充文旦農家：裴洛西訪台只為干預晶片產業、選舉造勢、撈金騙錢，造成文旦禁運中國，使家庭失去生計，導致台灣喪失海峽中線並危及和平。

4 The National Palace Museum, Taiwan plans to move the national treasures to the U.S. and Japan.
台灣故宮準備將國寶撤離至美國及日本

5 CCP: PLA ships are approaching Hualian Heping Power Plant and Taiwan's national warships.
中共：解放軍艦接近花蓮和平電廠及我國軍艦

6 Missiles are targeting the Taoyuan International Airport.
導彈擊中桃園機場

7 China plans to evacuate overseas Chinese from Taiwan.
中國將從台灣撤僑

8 The Taiwan government spent 94 million NTD on lobbying efforts to invite Pelosi to visit Taiwan.
台灣政府花 9,400 萬遊說裴洛西訪台

9 The departure of the USS Ronald Reagan indicated the abandonment of Taiwan and implicit approval of the CCP's lockdown of Taiwan.
美軍航空母艦雷根號跑走，是拋棄台灣，默認中共封鎖台灣

Include faulted contents 包含錯誤內容	Initiated by CCP 中共發起		
Unverifiable source 無法證實來源	Overgeneralization 以偏概全	Inappropriate causal relation 不當因果關係	
Unverifiable source 無法證實來源	Without evidence 沒有證據	Hacked account 受盜用帳號	
Include faulted contents 包含錯誤內容			
Include faulted contents 包含錯誤內容	Initiated by CCP 中共發起		
Include faulted contents 包含錯誤內容	Appeal to fear 訴諸恐懼		
Forged source 假造來源	Forged content 變造內容	Appeal to fear 訴諸恐懼	Pending judicial validation 尚待司法調查
Forged content 變造內容	Without evidence 沒有證據	Hacked account 受盜用帳號	
Insufficient evidences 證據不足	Overgeneralization 以偏概全	Appeal to fear 訴諸恐懼	America skepticism 疑美論

Source 資料來源 (14)

Type 1. Directly initiated by the CCP
類型一｜由中共直接發起

In the first type of information manipulation directly initiated by the CCP, the case of Nancy Pelosi's visit to Taiwan represents the largest-scale and highest-level manipulation, even acknowledged openly by CCP state media. We will analyze the CCP's official information manipulation process through the example of "SU-35 fighter jets crossing the Taiwan Strait."

在第一種由中共直接發起的訊息操作類型中，裴洛西來台的案例是操弄規模最大、層級最高，甚至中共官媒也公開承認的案例。我們藉由「蘇 35 共機穿越台灣海峽」這則資訊，來分析中共官方的訊息操弄過程：

Aug 2　8月2號

22:17　The Weibo account "玉渊谭天", an affiliated brand of CCP state media group, *China Media Group*, released the fake news at 22:17 PM on this day.

中共官媒集團「中央廣播電視總台」旗下品牌「玉渊谭天」於微博帳號當日 22:17 發布此假消息

22:18　CCP state media, Global Times, released the news "玉渊谭天": Su-35 Jets Were Sent to The Taiwan Strait.
— Subsequently, the Taiwanese news media ETtoday and United Daily News also had relevant news stories.

中共官媒「環球時報」發布報導「玉渊谭天：解放军空军苏 -35 战机穿越台湾海峡」——後續台灣新聞媒體 ETtoday、聯合新聞網也有相關報導

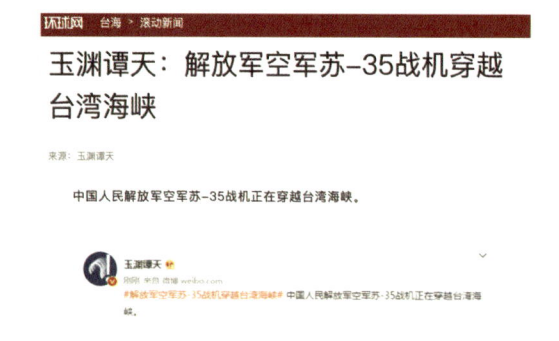

22:23 The initial Facebook post was posted by China V TV. Subsequently, various CCP state media also released relevant posts, including HK People's Daily, Macao Daily News, and HK Wen Wei Po.

在 Facebook 最早是由「中華微視」在 22:23 發布。而後，多個中共官媒陸續發佈相關貼文，包括「人民日報香港」、「澳門日報」、「香港文匯報」。

22:36 Six Facebook pages under the Want Want China Times Media Group umbrella, "無色覺醒," "大新聞大爆卦," Headlines Talk, Play It My Way, CTi TV News, and the Deep Throat News, initiated mass posting and broadcasted on CTi TV News: *Breaking News–As Nancy Pelosi's Visit to Taiwan Counts Down, Su-35 Jets Were Sent to The Taiwan Strait.*

旺旺中時集團旗下 6 個粉專「無色覺醒」、「大新聞大爆卦」、「頭條開講」、「正常發揮」、「快點 TV」和「新聞深喉嚨」群聚發文，傳播中天快點 TV 報導「快訊／裴洛西抵台倒數計時 解放軍空軍蘇 -35 戰機穿越台灣海峽」

22:44 Nancy Pelosi and the US Congressional Delegation Arrives in Taiwan.

裴洛西及眾議院訪問團抵達台灣

Aug 7　8月7號

CCP state media CCTV reports, Revealing Pelosi: "玉淵譚天" Three Consecutive Posts!, claiming "玉淵譚天" as the "China Media Group's brand for opinion," detailing the impact of "玉淵譚天," "協同" and "China Media Group" on the opinions of international affairs inside China.

中共官媒「央視」報導「揭底佩洛西：玉淵譚天三連發！」，稱「玉淵譚天」為「总台言论评论品牌」，詳述「玉淵譚天」「協同」「总台」影響中國國內海外輿論。

23:20 The Ministry of National Defense of Taiwan published a press release clarifying that the earlier news report was false.

我國國防部發布新聞稿，澄清此事並非事實

Source 資料來源（15）

Type 2. Posting on social media by using a stolen account
類型二│透過盜用帳號於社交平台發文

Next, let's examine the second pattern, which involves posting through hijacked accounts and then amplifying through official media citations. Here, we'll use the example of "Taiwan government spends 94 million lobbying for Pelosi's visit" to analyze the manipulation process:

接著,我們來看第二種模式,即是透過盜用帳號發文,再以官媒引用擴大的方式,這邊我們已「台灣政府花 9,400 萬遊說裴洛西訪台」的訊息為例,分析操弄過程:

Aug 2　8 月 2 號

22:44　Nancy Pelosi and the US Congressional Delegation Arrives in Taiwan.

　　　　裴洛西及眾議院訪問團抵達臺灣。

23:58　In a post on Facebook page "The Thinker Lee," the author expressed the opinion that Pelosi's visit to Taiwan was "the DPP administration spent 94 million NTD on lobbying efforts to invite Pelosi to visit Taiwan and bet on Taiwanese people's life."

　　　　Facebook 「李勝峯 理性鋒爆」發文表示裴洛西訪台是「民進黨花了 9400 萬稅金遊說,以台灣人民身家性命為籌碼,邀請裴洛西訪台」。

Aug 4　8 月 4 號

10:35　Account "home12196" posted on the Gossip Page: "Taiwan lobbied Pelosi and paid 94 million NTD" with a forged picture that declared that it is from the shortened URL of the US Department of Justice. On the same-day afternoon, the account user reported to the police that the account had been hacked. In the afternoon, the Ministry of Foreign Affairs condemned the false message.

　　　　home12196 在八卦版板發文「我國遊說裴洛西付費 9400 萬」附上宣稱來自美國司法部外國代理人登記網站短網址的變造圖片。當日下午該帳號持有者亦向警方報案,表示帳號被盜。

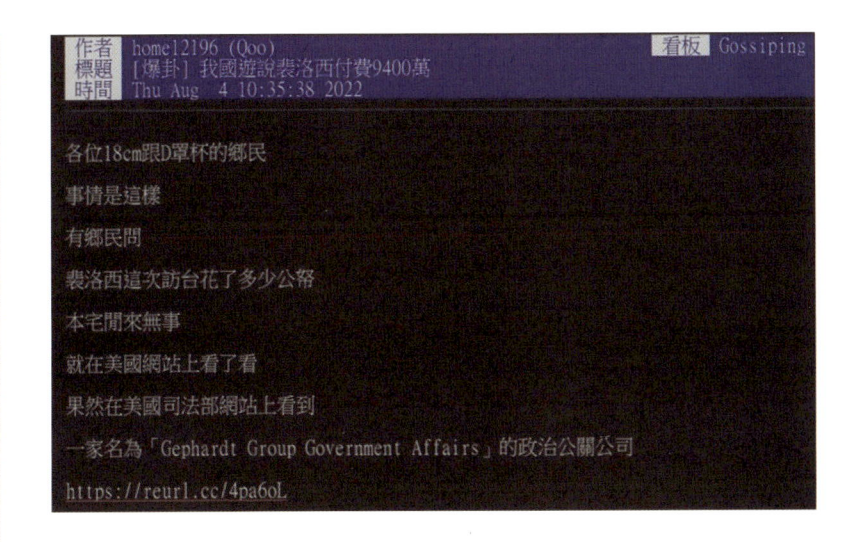

In the afternoon, the Ministry of Foreign Affairs condemned the false message.

下午,外交部駁斥此為錯誤訊息。

16:08 CCP state media Tai-Hai Net quoted an original post from PTT and headlined news stories, "Scoops from Taiwanese Media." On the same day, taiwan.cn, ifeng–Taiwan channel, The Paper, and the China Review News Agency Limited, among others, collaborated in spreading this discourse.

中共官媒「台海網」引用了PTT原文「台媒爆料」為題發佈新聞,當天另有「中國台灣網」、「鳳凰網_台灣」、「澎湃新聞」及「台灣中評網」等多家官媒協力傳播此論述。

CTi News' "快點TV" headlined an article: "Taiwan-US Relations at All-Time High? Third Party Reveals Shocking Behind-the-Scenes DPP 'Spending of 94 Million NTD' on Lobbying Nancy Pelosi." On the same day, Facebook pages, "正常發揮," "無色覺醒," "大新聞大爆卦," and "頭條開講" initiated mass posting.

「中天快點TV」發表標題「台美關係史上最好?他曝光驚人內幕…民進黨竟『花9400萬』遊說裴洛西」文章,並在當日18:15由粉專「正常發揮」、「無色覺醒」、「大新聞大爆卦」及「頭條開講」群聚發文。

YouTube account "Bit King REAL Taiwan's true politics" video titled, "Too Late to Retreat?! CCP Will Comprehensively Upgrade! Taiwan Exports at Risk of Comprehensive Lockdown?!" On the next day, Facebook pages "台灣人民心聲分享粉專," "國際新聞分享粉專," and "直播分享美德" initiated mass posting.

Youtube帳號「Bit King比特王出任務」的影片「回不去了!?中共將全面升級!台灣出口面臨全面封鎖!?」在隔日由「台灣人民心聲分享粉專」、「國際新聞分享粉專」及「直播分享美德」群聚發文。

Source 資料來源 (15)

Case two:
TSMC linked to suspected US Skepticism
案例二：台積電與疑美論

TSMC has been a highly regarded international enterprise in recent years, often referred to as the "pride of Taiwan.It has also become a focal point for various conspiracy theories related to the U.S., leading to widespread discussion.

In May 11, 2021, the CCP's state media outlet Huaxia Jingwei started spreading doubts about TSMC's plan to set up a factory in the U.S., through its programs. This indicates that the CCP's state media may have guided this entire discussion. In 2022, US Skepticism related to TSMC peaked, two suspicious narratives emerged: one claimed that TSMC's move to the U.S. was part of America's plan to hollow out Taiwan, and the other suggested that during a war, the U.S. would evacuate TSMC engineers and then use a scorched-earth tactic to destroy

	Establishing TSMC plants in the U.S. is the U.S. draining resources from Taiwan 可疑論述流行期間		China participation 中國參與
1	Establishing TSMC plants in the U.S. is the U.S. draining resources from Taiwan 台積電赴美設廠是美國掏空台灣	2021/5-2022/1-11	Initiator 發起
2	Establishing TSMC plants in the U.S. is a decision coerced by the U.S. with the DPP having no power to refuse. 台積電赴美設廠是受到美國脅迫，民進黨政府無力阻止	2021/10-2022/1-11	Initiator 發起
3	When the war erupts, the U.S. will implement a scorched-earth policy that devastates TSMC. 開戰時，美國會採取焦土戰術，摧毀台積電	2021/10-2022/1	Amplified the reach 放大
4	When the war erupts, the U.S. will evacuate TSMC engineers, implementing a scorched-earth policy that devastates Taiwan. 開戰時，美國會撤離台積電工程師，採取焦土戰術，摧毀台灣	2021/10-2022/5-11	Initiator 發起
5	The DPP administration is aiding the U.S. in selling out TSMC, abandoning Taiwan. 民進黨政府協助美國出賣台積電，放棄台灣	2022/8-11	Amplified the reach 放大
6	The DPP administration is aiding the U.S. in selling out TSMC, abandoning Taiwan, and planning to flee with the U.S. Navy when war erupts. 民進黨政府協助美國出賣台積電，放棄台灣，開戰時逃到美軍航空母艦上	2022/11	Amplified the reach 放大
7	China plans to evacuate overseas Chinese from Taiwan 中國將從台灣撤僑	2022/11	Amplified the reach 放大

Taiwan. These narratives saw an unusual surge in posts before the local elections in Taiwan in November 2022.This suggests a certain level of coordination, known as coordinated inauthentic behavior.

台積電是近年來全球知名的跨國大企業,甚至被稱之為台灣之光。所以台積電與疑美論連結,也帶來了更大的討論熱度。

早在 2021 年 5 月,中共官媒華夏經緯網就透過旗下節目開始散佈台積電赴美設廠,是美國要拋棄台灣,顯示中共官媒可能引導了輿論走向。 2022 年是台積電疑美論的高峰期,出現了兩個可疑論述,第一個是台積電赴美國設廠,是美國要掏空台灣;以及開戰後美國撤離台積電工程師,會用焦土戰術摧毀台灣,而這些論述在 2022 年 11 月台灣地方選舉前,出現了不尋常的群聚發文現象,可以猜測應該有一定程度的協同性。

Taiwan participation 台灣參與	America skepticism classifications 疑美論分類	Message Credibility Assessment 訊息可信度
Amplified the reach 放大	Frenemy 假朋友	Insufficient evidences 證據不足
Amplified the reach 放大	Frenemy 假朋友	Appeal to emotion 訴諸情緒
Initiator 發起	Destroying Taiwan 毀臺	Forged contents 變造內容
Amplified the reach 放大	Destroying Taiwan 毀臺	Forged contents 變造內容 / Overgeneralization 以偏概全 / Appeal to emotion 訴諸情緒 / Mass posting 群聚發文
Initiator 發起	Conspirer 共謀	Inappropriate causal relation 不當因果關係
Initiator 發起	Conspirer 共謀	Insufficient evidences 證據不足 / Mass posting 群聚發文
Initiator 發起	Conspirer 共謀	Insufficient evidences 證據不足

Source 資料來源 (16)

Chapter 1 | A battlefield without gunpowder: China's influence operations against Taiwan
沒有煙硝的戰場：中國對臺灣影響力行動

Nov 16　11月16日

Content farm posts
內容農場發文

> **The U.S. has already gradually abandoned Taiwan**
> 美國已開始逐步放棄台灣

Skepticism Discourse 1
可疑論述 1

2021.5 - 2022.1-11

Establishing TSMC Plants in the U.S. Is the U.S. Draining Resources from Taiwan
台積電赴美設廠是美國掏空台灣

- In 2021, CCP's state media has mentioned the U.S. "draining resources from Taiwan"

- In March, 2022, Mike Pompeo's visit in Taiwan was deemed as "draining resources from Taiwan"

  - From April to June, the "draining resources from TSMC" discourse has been used to support "draining resources from Taiwan." First initiated by Tang Hsiang-Lung, Julian Kuo's opinion was widely circulated.
  - In August, Nancy Pelosi visited Taiwan and the CHIPS Act for America was published, the "draining resources from Taiwan" hypothesis continued to circulate.
  - <u>In November</u>, the focus of the discourse was transitioned to pointing Taiwan government as the "accomplice" and "stooge." <u>The mass posting has amplified the "Say Goodbye to Taiwan" hypothesis</u>

- 2021 年中共官媒即提及美國「掏空台灣」

- 2022 年 3 月龐培歐訪台亦為「掏空台灣」

  - 4-6 月論述以「掏空台積電」實現「掏空台灣」唐湘龍最早、郭正亮言論多獲轉傳

  - 8 月裴洛西訪台、美國晶片法案，「掏空台灣」論述持續傳播

  - <u>11 月</u>論述焦點轉至台灣政府是「幫凶」「走狗」<u>群聚發文放大美國「棄台論」</u>

Nov 17　11月17日
11:34 - 11:35 AM

Rapid mass posting
短時間內群聚發文

- Overseas Chinese Alliance Info
- Concern Malaysia
- Current Affair Express
- Descendants of Dragon
- True Lies
- Focus of the Day
- Pls Like if you are earth people
- China Rises
- Chinese Rising
- The Belt and Road China Revitalization
……

- 海外華人同盟資訊
- 关心大马事
- 時事快遞
- 龍的傳人
- 真政內幕
- 今日焦點
- 是地球人就请按赞
- 中國崛起
- 中華民族站起來了
- 一帶一路 中國復興
……

Nov 25 11月25日

Content farm posts
內容農場發文

Nov 26 11月26日

Election day
選舉日

Nov 28 11月28日
17:19 - 17:20

Rapid mass posting
短時間內群聚發文

"U.S's scorched-earth policy Destroying Taiwan's key infrastructures
美方焦土戰摧毀島內所有關鍵設施

Skepticism Discourse 4
可疑論述 4

2022.1-11

When the war erupts, the U.S. will evacuate TSMC engineers, implementing a scorched-earth policy that devastates Taiwan.
開戰時，美國會撤離台積電工程師，採焦土戰術摧毀台灣

In January, China Times misinterpreted U.S. scholar's writing submission and put forward the "destroying TSMC" hypothesis.

In May, CCP's state media fabricated expert opinions from U.S. scholars, which were echoed by CCP's official government sources. The forged contents were then disseminated into Taiwan, giving rise to the "U.S.'s Taiwan Destroy" hypothesis based on the "destroying TSMC" premise.

In October, CCP's state media continued to cooperate with spreading the opinions of that the U.S. was "evacuating TSMC engineers" and "destroying TSMC," which was exclusively reported in the CTi News' Facebook page, in combination with sensational contents in China Times and the United Daily News associated with the U.S.'s "Taiwan Destroy" hypothesis.

In November, mass posting emerged to amplify the statement of the "U.S.'s scorched-earth policy."

1月《中時》錯誤詮釋美國學者投書，提出「摧毀台積電」

5月中共官媒變造美國學者專家意見，中共官方呼應，變造內容進入台灣，以「摧毀台積電」創造「美國毀台論」

10月中共官媒持續協力傳播美國「撤離台積電工程師」、「摧毀台積電」，中天粉專分享自家報導與《中時》、《聯合》聳動內容，連結棄台論

11月出現群聚發文放大「美國焦土戰」說法

- Overseas Chinese Alliance Info
- Concern Malaysia
- Descendants of Dragon
- True Lies
- Focus of the Day
- Pls Like if you are earth people
- China Rises
- Chinese Rising
- The Belt and Road China Revitalization
- What you care about is the hot news
……

- 海外華人同盟資訊
- 关心大马事
- 龍的傳人
- 真政內幕
- 今日焦點
- 是地球人就请按赞
- 中國崛起
- 中華民族站起來了
- 一帶一路 中國復興
- 你關心的 才是頭條
……

Source 資料來源（16）

In our research, we observed that these fan pages played a role akin to fertilizing. Fertilizing here means that based on the quantity of posts spread on Facebook, we found that when a message appears extensively, it can effectively drive up the number of likes within two hours. Essentially, for these content farms, the immediate visibility of their posts may not be their primary concern. Instead, by mass-posting, they mislead Facebook's algorithm into thinking the topic is significant. Subsequently, within two hours, their posts containing manipulated information may generate more discussion. This underscores how content farms can pose a potential hazard.

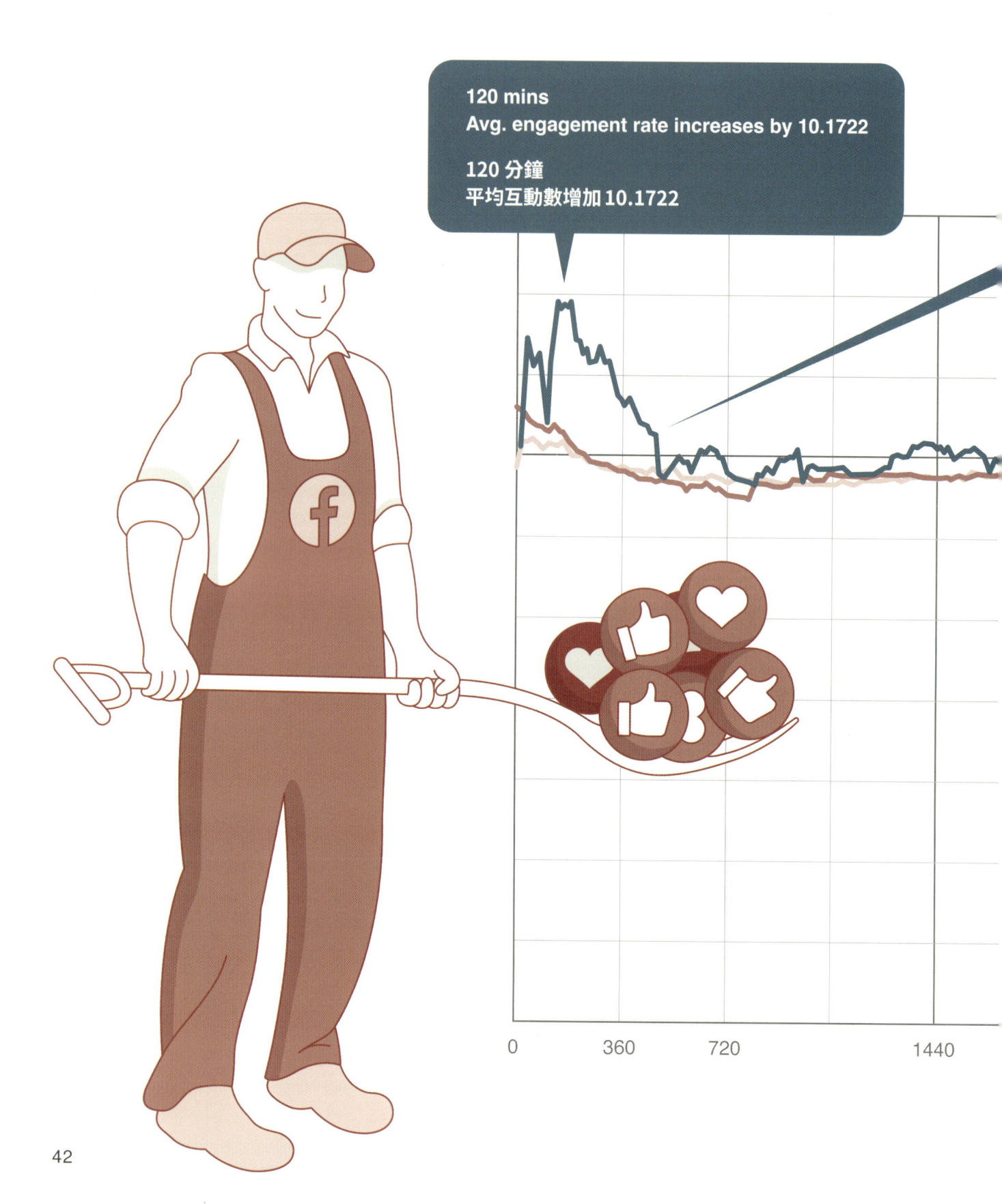

120 mins
Avg. engagement rate increases by 10.1722

120 分鐘
平均互動數增加 10.1722

而在我們的研究當中可以發現到，這些粉專所扮演的可以說是施肥的角色。施肥的意思是，我們從 Facebook 傳播的數量當中發現，當今天這個訊息大量出現之後，在兩個小時內，可以有效的帶動按讚的數量，也就是說，對這些內容農場來講，他們其實並不真的在意當下發文有沒有被人看到，而是透過大量的發文，誤導 Facebook 的演算法以為這是一個重大的議題，隨後在兩個小時之後，他們所發布的、帶有資訊操弄的內容，可能就會引起更多的討論，而這也是內容農場可能是一種危害的原因。

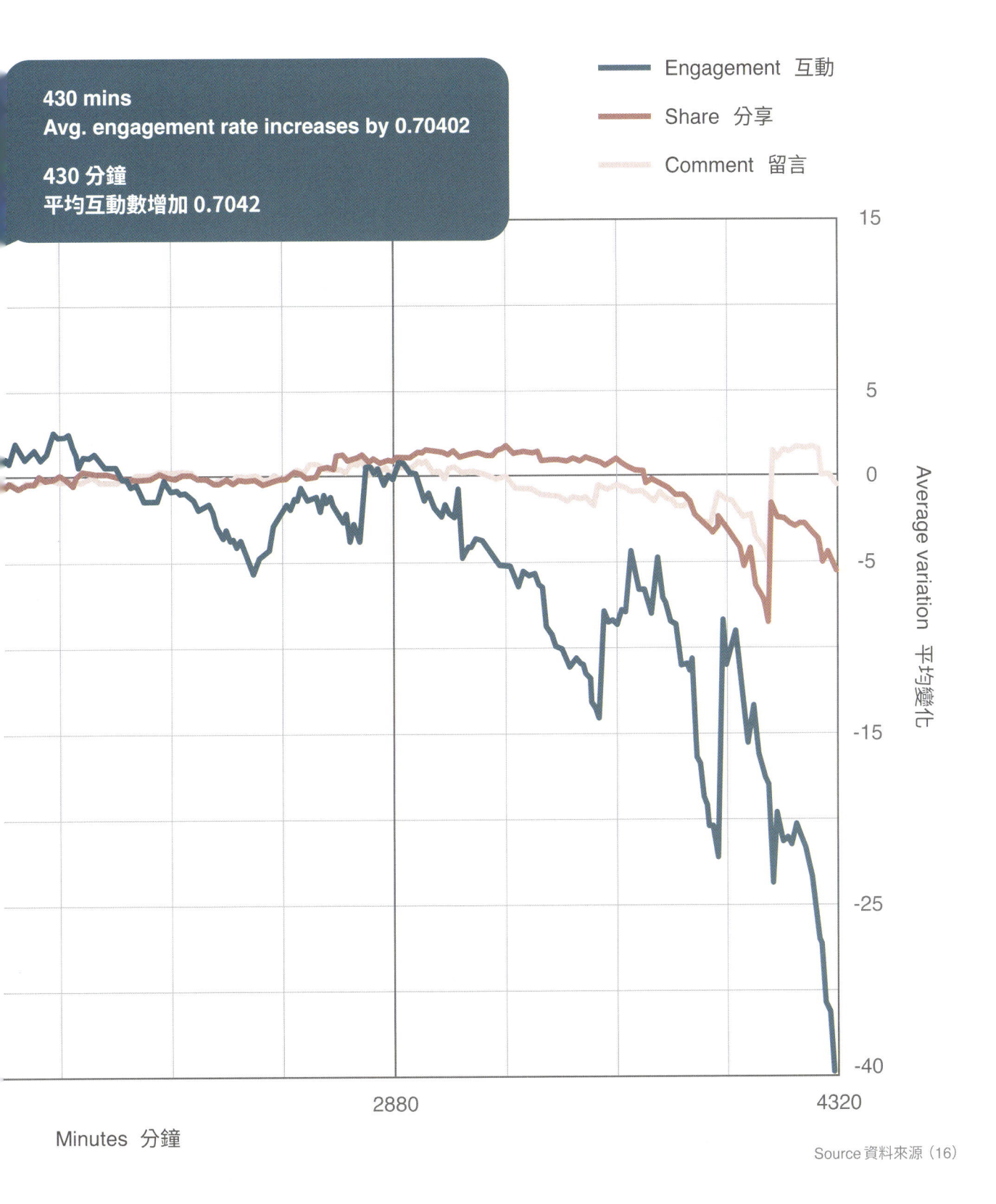

430 mins
Avg. engagement rate increases by 0.70402

430 分鐘
平均互動數增加 0.7042

Engagement 互動
Share 分享
Comment 留言

Average variation 平均變化

Minutes 分鐘

Source 資料來源（16）

Case three: biological weapons
案例三：生物戰劑

The third case occurred on July 9, 2023, when United Daily News exclusively reported that the United States intended to establish a P4 laboratory in Taiwan to develop biological weapons. They even presented meeting records indicating discussions within the DPP government. This immediately sparked protests from various Taiwanese government agencies, including the Ministry of National Defense and the Executive Yuan, with even the Presidential Office issuing direct clarifications that this was false information. However, according to our data, the discussion about biological weapons had actually been incubated by CCP officials for three to four years. Through this process, we can see how Chinese officials gradually developed such false information.

第三個案例，是在 2023 年 7 月 9 號，聯合報獨家爆料，宣稱美國要台灣設立 P4 實驗室，開發生物戰劑，甚至提出了會議紀錄，顯示民進黨政府的確有開會討論，這當然立刻引起了民進黨政府，包含各個行政機關從國防部到行政院的抗議，甚至總統府都直接出來澄清，這是不存在的假訊息。

但根據我們的資料顯示，事實上這個生物武器的討論，其實已經是中共官方，醞釀了三四年的討論，透過這個過程，我們可以看到中國官方是如何逐漸發展這樣的假訊息。

Joyce Huang forged Reuters' reports:
"The U.S. company Academi is the secret developer behind the UB-612 vaccine," the U.S. and Japan engage in biological weapon development targeting China.

黃智賢變造路透社報導：
「美國黑水公司是聯亞疫苗的幕後老闆」，美國、日本針對中國研究生化武器。

Hua Chunying, spokesperson of the Ministry of Foreign Affairs of China, states:
"The U.S. has established 16 biology labs in Ukraine."

中國外交部發言人华春莹：
「美国在乌克兰设立有 16 家生物实验室」。

The Office of the President, Ministry of National Defense, Ministry of Foreign Affairs, and AIT officially debunk the rumor in succession.

總統府、國防部、外交部、AIT 陸續聲明闢謠

United Daily News reveals:
"The Complete Meeting Minute of the South China Sea Conference"

聯合報報導公布「南海工作會議紀錄全文」

The Office of the President: TDPO has ratified that the official document was forged, urging United Daily News to immediately rectify and remove the untruthful reports.

總統府：北檢證實文件造假，呼籲《聯合報》應立即更正並撤除不實報導

Real China: The Communist Party and the People's Liberation Army under Xi Jinping
解密中國：習近平統治下的共產黨與解放軍

2020. 03. 12.

Zhao Lijian, spokesperson of the Ministry of Foreign Affairs of China, retweeted the video and commented that "the Covid-19 virus originated in the United States and was then brought to China by the U.S. military."

中國外交部發言人趙立堅在推特轉發影片並評論，稱「COVID-19 病毒是美國發源，再由美軍帶入中國。」

2021. 06. 13.

2022. 03. 08.

Zhao Lijian, spokesperson of the Ministry of Foreign Affairs of China, states:
"The U.S. Department of Defense has control over 336 biology labs in 30 countries globally. You heard it right."

中國外交部發言人趙立堅：
「美国国防部在全球 30 个国家控制了 336 个生物实验室。336，你没有听错」。

2022. 05. 08.

United Daily News' exclusive reports:
"The U.S. Plans P4 Labs in Taiwan for Biological Weapons Development? Documents Reveal Evidences of DPP's Meeting Minute"
"From Anti-Biological Weapons to Covertly Promoting Development. DPP's Blind US Favorability Abandons Conscience."

2023. 07. 09.

聯合報獨家爆料：
「美要台灣設 P4 實驗室開發生物戰劑？文件顯示民進黨政府曾開會討論」
「從反生物戰劑到秘密推動研發，民進黨盲目親美毀棄良知」

2023. 07. 12.

2023. 07. 18.

2023. 09. 05.

Justin Wu, Hsieh Pei-fen, and Attorney Huang Di-ying reported to TDPO (Taiwan Taipei District Prosecutors Office) that the publication falsified information and that the official document was forged.

吳崢、謝佩芬及律師黃帝穎向北檢告發業務登載不實、變造偽造公文書

45

Chapter 2

Through the red lens:
an analysis of the CCP's political operations
紅色透視鏡：中共政治運作解析

The political system of authoritarian countries is vastly different from that of democratic countries. Therefore, the researcher at the Institute of Political Science at Academia Sinica, Wen-Hsuan Tsai, is invited to introduce the operational model of the CCP's party and government organizations. This aims to establish a solid knowledge foundation for journalists to "understand China."

The characteristic of the CCP's political operation and decision-making is "party-led governance," where the Party is above the government. At the same time, the phenomenon of "one institution, two nameplates" is common. For example, the Central Propaganda Department and the State Council Information Office are staffed by the same people. Since Xi Jinping came to power in 2012, he has changed the collective decision-making practice within the CCP, re-emphasizing party-led governance through measures such as ideological education, organizational reform, and disciplinary inspections. Xi Jinping holds multiple titles, including General Secretary of the CCP, Chairman of the Central Military Commission, and President of the state, centralizing power in his hands.

In this course, besides explaining how these complex institutions operate, a chronological table of major events will also be used to illustrate Xi Jinping's institutional consolidation of power since taking office. This helps journalists clearly understand the trajectory of the CCP's power operation, offering a comprehensive view of the government and Party organizations. At the same time, based on this knowledge, they can predict the succession issues of the CCP's regime.

Keywords: party-led government, institutionalized centralization

威權國家的政治體制與民主國家大相逕庭，因此，央廣邀請中研院政治所蔡文軒研究員，介紹中共黨政組織的運作模式，就是在為新聞工作者「認識中國」建立良好的知識基礎。

中共政治運作與決策的特色為「以黨領政」，黨高於政府；與此同時，「一個機構兩塊招牌」是常見現象，例如中共中央對外宣傳辦公室，同一批人也組成國務院新聞辦公室。2012年習近平上臺後，改變中共集體決策的慣例，重新加強以黨領政，以思想教育、組織改革、紀律檢查等措施。習近平同時是中共中央總書記、軍委主席與國家主席，權力集於一身。

在本課程中，除了解說這些複雜的機構如何運作，也會以大事記年表，說明習近平上任後的制度性集權手段，讓新聞工作者清楚看出中共權力運行的軌跡，一窺中共政府與黨組織的全貌，同時根據這些知識，預判中共的政權接班問題。

關鍵字：以黨領政、制度性集權

2-1
The mysterious Chinese government & party organizations
紅色神秘的中國政府與黨組織

Introduction to the organization of the Chinese communist party
中國共產黨組織介紹

China is a one-party state primarily governed by the political elites within the Chinese Communist Party (CCP). The party's power structure is hierarchical, resembling a pyramid. The representatives of each higher level are elected by members of the lower level, and the top leader is the General Secretary of the CCP.

From this progressive, tiered system, it becomes evident that the real power within the CCP is held by Politburo members and the Politburo Standing Committee members at the top of the pyramid. This constitutes the core institution of the Chinese Communist Party.

中國是一黨專政、以黨領政的威權國家,由中國共產黨內部的政治菁英來主導國家運作。黨內的權力結構是金字塔型,低一層級成員選出上一層級之代表,最上層即是中國共產黨的「總書記」。從這樣的層層遞進的模式來看,可以發現中國共產黨的實際權力,是掌握在金字塔頂端的政治局委員跟政治局常委手中,這就是中國共產黨最核心的權力機構。而中國共產黨的總書記也是政治局常委之一,是實際上的中國最高領導人,而非民主國家所以為的國家主席。

Meets about once a week, not necessarily public.
約每週召開一次,會議不一定公開

Meets about once a month.
約 1 個月召開一次

At least one meeting/year.
1 年至少召開一次

Meets every five years.
5 年召開一次

Real China: The Communist Party and the People's Liberation Army under Xi Jinping
解密中國：習近平統治下的共產黨與解放軍

General secretary
總書記

Politburo Standing Committee: 7 members
中央政治局常務委員 7 人

CCP Politburo: 25 members
中央政治局委員 25 人

CCP Central Committee
中央委員會

Central Committee: 205 members
中央委員 205 人

Discipline Inspection Committee: 338 members
中央紀律委員 338 人

CCP National Congress: 2,296 members(Top 20)
全國黨代表大會 2,296 人

~96.71M CCP members nationwide
全國共產黨黨員約 9,671 萬人

49

Chapter 2 | Through the red lens: an analysis of the CCP's political operations
紅色透視鏡：中共政治運作解析

Key leadership positions and figures in the CCP
中國共產黨的主要領導職位與人物

Ranking 排名		Party positions 黨職	Public positions 公職
1	 **Xi Jinping** 習近平	General Secretary of the Central Committee / Chairman of the Central Military Commission 中央總書記 / 中共中央軍委主席	President of the State / Chairman of the Central Military Commission 國家主席 / 中國中央軍委主席
2	 **Li Qiang** 李　強	Secretary of the State Council Party Group 國務院黨組書記	Premier of the State Council 國務院總理
3	 **Zhao Leji** 趙樂際	Secretary of the NPC Standing Committee Party Group 全國人大常委會黨組書記	Chairman of the NPC Standing Committee 全國人大常委會委員長
4	 **Wang Huning** 王滬寧	Secretary of the National Committee of the Chinese Party Group 全國政協黨組書記	Chairman of the National Committee of the Chinese People's Political Consultative Conference (CPPCC) 全國政協主席
5	 **Cai Qi** 蔡　奇	Senior Secretary of the CCP Secretariat / Director of the CCP General Office / Secretary of the Central and State Organs Work Committee / Director of the General Secretary's Office 中央書記處書記（第1）/ 中央辦公廳主任 / 中央和國家機關工委書記 / 中央總書記辦公室主任	Director of the Office of the President 國家主席辦公室主任
6	 **Ding Xuexiang** 丁薛祥	Deputy Secretary of the State Council Party Group 國務院黨組副書記	Senior Vice Premier of the State Council 國務院副總理（排名第1）
7	 **Li Xi** 李　希	Secretary of the Central Commission for Discipline Inspection(CCDI) 中央紀委書記	

這裡提供的範例具時效性內容

The Situation of the 20th National Congress 二十大情形	Explanation of the composition of the Politburo and the Politburo Standing Committee members. 政治局及政治局常委人員組成說明
Politburo Standing Committee 政治局常委	Historically, the number of Standing Committee members has ranged from 5 to 9. During the tenure of the former General Secretary Hu Jintao, the Politburo Standing Committee had 9 members. After Xi Jinping took office, the number of Standing Committee members was reduced to 7. 歷史上常委人數 5-9 人不等，前任總書記胡錦濤時期，政治局常委為 9 人，習近平上任後常委減至 7 人。
Politburo Members 政治局委員	● The Politburo typically consists of 25 members, including personnel from the Party apparatus, the National People's Congress, the State Council, the military, the Chinese People's Political Consultative Conference, and local systems. There are customary positions that qualify for Politburo membership. ● Besides General Secretary Xi Jinping, the Party apparatus has 6 members; the State Council includes 5 members (the Premier and Vice Premiers); local Party Secretaries account for 6 members; the National People's Congress has 2 members (the Chairperson and a Vice Chairperson); the Central Military Commission has 2 Vice-Chairpersons; and the Chinese People's Political Consultative Conference has 1 Chairperson. ● 通常由 25 人組成，包括黨務、人大、國務院、軍隊、政協、地方等系統人員，可入政治局委員的職位亦有慣例。 ● 除中央總書記習近平外，黨務系統共計 6 人；國務院正副總理 5 人，地方書記 6 人，全國人大正副委員長 2 人，軍委副主席 2 人，全國政協主席 1 人。

Through the explanation of the power structure and organizational model above, we can understand that the real power of the Chinese Communist Party is held by the Politburo and the Politburo Standing Committee. The Politburo and the Politburo Standing Committee elected after the 20th National Congress of the Chinese Communist Party in 2022 represent the current power core of the CCP. It is evident that these seven members operate with Xi Jinping as the core, while the other six carries different works. This marks a significant departure from the era of Hu Jintao, where power among the Standing Committee members was relatively balanced.

透過前頁權力架構與組織模式的說明，我們可以了解，中國共產黨實際上的權力核心集中在政治局及政治局常委手中，而 2022 年第二十屆全國黨代表大會（二十大）所選出的政治局常委會七位常委，即是目前中國共產黨的重要人物。我們可以看到，七位常委以習近平為核心來運作，其他六人分管不同的業務。這跟胡錦濤時期，政治局常委之間權力分配較為平衡的狀況，有很大不同。

China's party-state system
中國的黨政體制

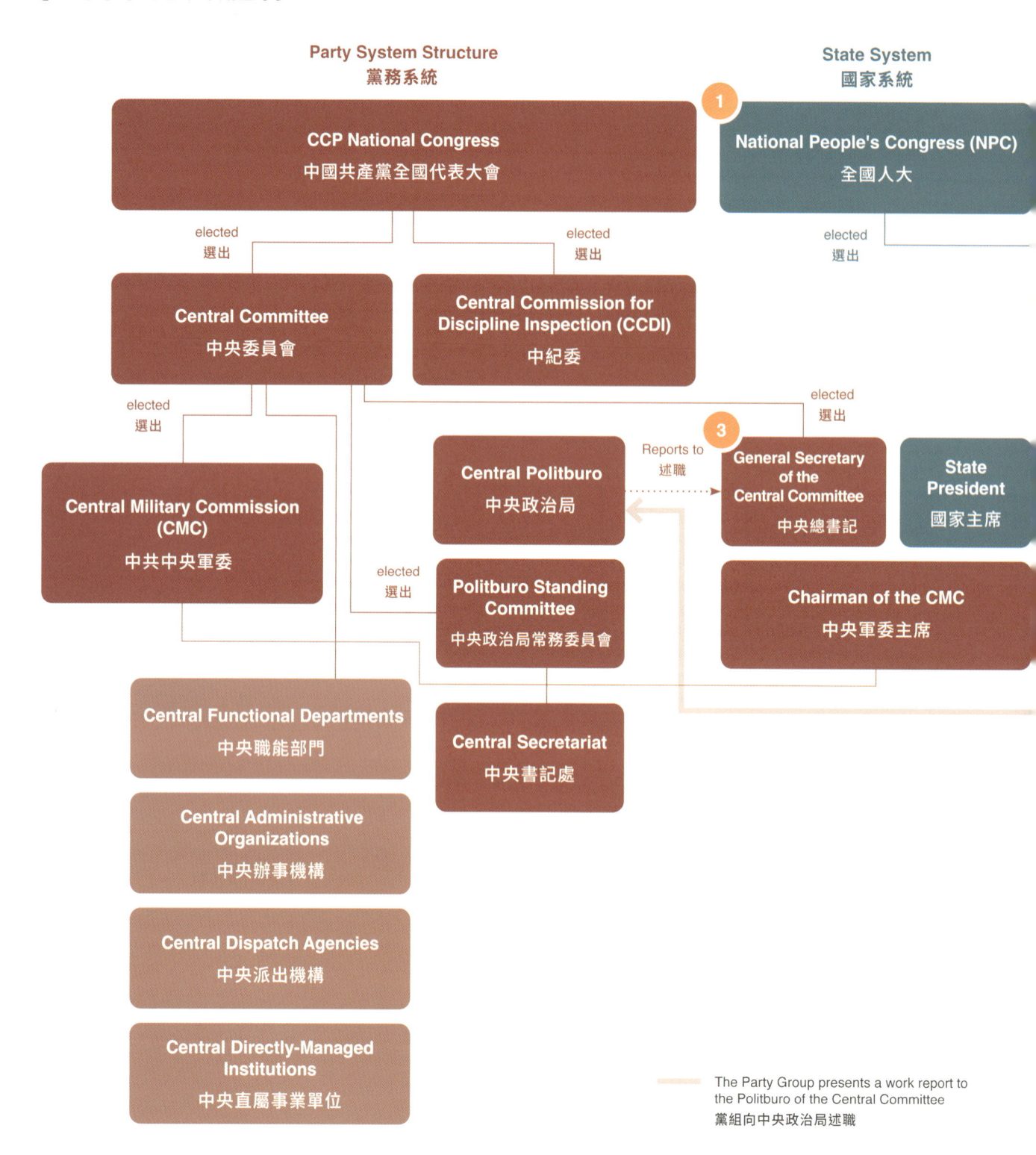

Party System Structure 黨務系統 | State System 國家系統

```
CCP National Congress                           National People's Congress (NPC)
中國共產黨全國代表大會                              全國人大
        │ elected 選出                                    │ elected 選出
        ├──────────────────┐
Central Committee      Central Commission for
中央委員會              Discipline Inspection (CCDI)
                       中紀委
        │ elected 選出
        ├─── Central Military Commission (CMC) 中共中央軍委
        │
        ├─── Central Politburo 中央政治局  ⟶ Reports to 述職 ⟶  General Secretary of the Central Committee 中央總書記  │  State President 國家主席
        │                                                                                                              │
        ├─── Politburo Standing Committee 中央政治局常務委員會                                Chairman of the CMC 中央軍委主席
        │
        ├─── Central Functional Departments 中央職能部門
        ├─── Central Secretariat 中央書記處
        ├─── Central Administrative Organizations 中央辦事機構
        ├─── Central Dispatch Agencies 中央派出機構
        └─── Central Directly-Managed Institutions 中央直屬事業單位
```

The Party Group presents a work report to the Politburo of the Central Committee
黨組向中央政治局述職

During Hu Jintao's tenure, the national system maintained relative independence and decision-making authority compared to the Party system. However, under Xi Jinping, he has largely weakened the decision-making authority and resources of the State Council and related government departments. This means that the power of the national system is rapidly declining, with the Party now controlling all affairs—economy, corporate, society, and technology. The Party is omnipresent and all-encompassing.

Chart

② Chinese People's Political Consultative Conference (CPPCC) Party Group
全國政協黨組

NPC Standing Committee Party Group
人大常委會黨組

State Council Party Group
國務院黨組

Supreme People's Procuratorate Party Group
最高人民檢察院黨組

Supreme People's Court Party Group
最高人民法院黨組

National Supervisory Commission
國家監察委員會

CMC
中央軍事委員會

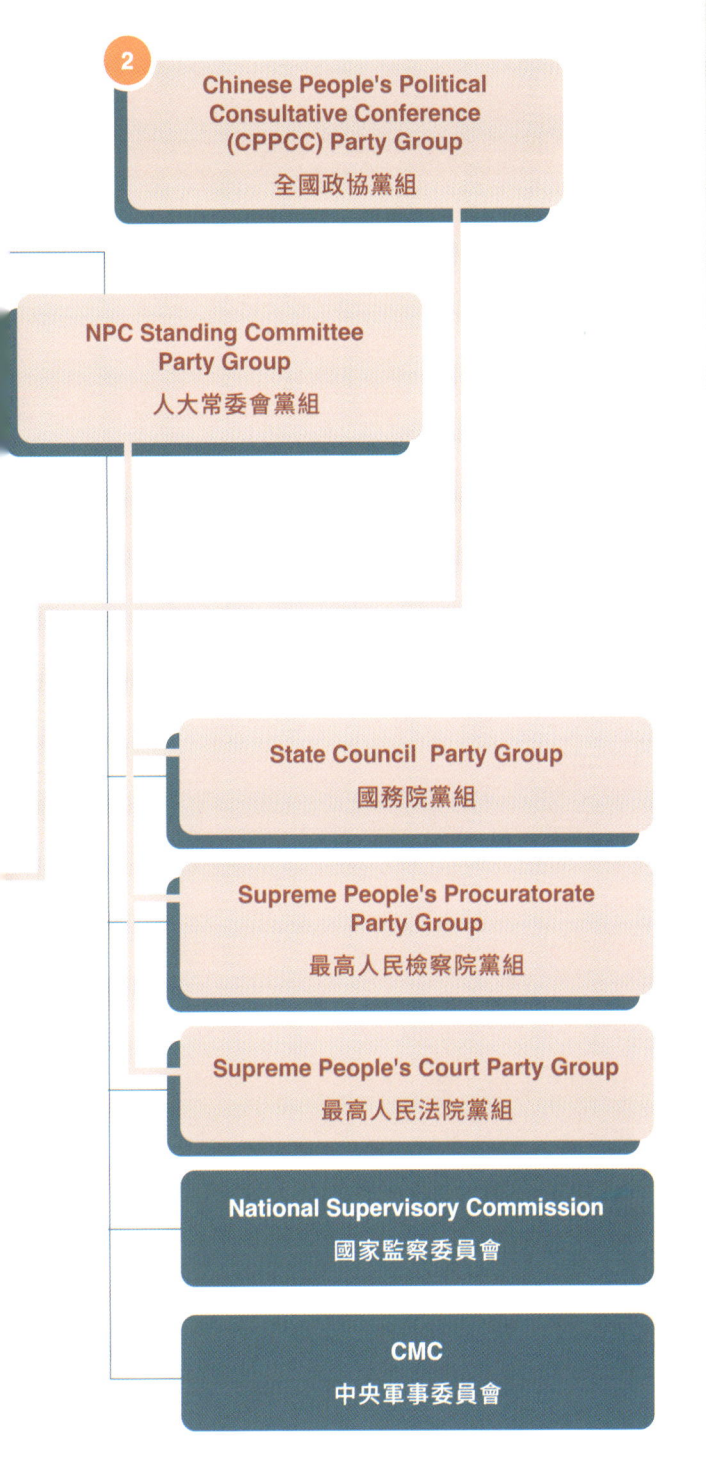

① The NPC primarily functions in legislation, akin to the legislative branch or parliament in democratic nations. However, in communist countries, the legislative body does not possess independent legislative power and often operates under party control.

主要職能是立法，相當於立法院，但是在共產黨國家當中，立法機構並沒有獨立的立法權，很多情況還是聽從黨的控制。

② The CPPCC oversees united front work. By observing changes in its division of responsibilities, we can grasp the future direction of the Chinese Communist Party's united front strategies.

「全國政協」就是掌管統戰的部門，我們從全國政協裡分管事務的增減狀況，就能理解中國共產黨的未來統戰方向。

③ Additionally, in the center of the chart, there are three very important positions: the General Secretary, the State President, and the Chairman of the Central Military Commission. These three positions represent the highest leaders of the Party, the state, and the military, respectively, and are all currently held by Xi Jinping.

總書記、國家主席以及中央軍委主席，這三個職位分別代表黨、政、軍的最高領導人物，目前都是由習近平所擔任。

在過去的胡錦濤時期，國家系統相對於黨務系統，仍有相對的獨立性與決策權。但在習近平時期，國務院與相關政府部門的決策權與資源，都被習近平用各式各樣的委員會架空，亦即國家系統完全成為黨的附屬，由黨控制了所有的事務。黨管經濟、黨管企業、黨管社會、黨管科技、黨無所不在、無所不包。

2-2
Evolution of a dictator: Xi's institutional centralization of power
獨裁者的進化：習近平與制度化集權

How did Xi Jinping consolidate power?
習近平如何集權？

Centralization of personal power

權力向習近平一人集中

During Xi Jinping's era, the relationship between the Party and the government was mainly characterized by the Party's absorption, weakening, and control over government organizations. Additionally, Xi Jinping consolidates personal power as the supreme leader in the Party, government, and military. This personal consolidation of power evokes comparisons with Mao Zedong, but the key distinction lies in their methods: Mao centralized power through mass movements and large-scale political purges. In contrast, Xi Jinping's power consolidation largely involves "institutionalizing centralization," establishing a foundation of personal authority through institutional mechanisms.

習近平時期的黨政關係，主要體現在黨對政府組織的吸納、弱化與控制，以及習近平一人身兼黨政軍最高領導人物的個人集權情形。這種個人集權情形，讓很多人想到毛澤東，但是習近平跟毛澤東之間的最大不同在於，毛澤東是透過群眾運動、透過大規模的政治整肅運動，來鞏固個人權力；但是習近平的權力集中方式，很大程度是透過「建立制度」來打造個人集權基礎，也就是這邊所說的「制度化集權」模式。

Xi Jinping has primarily consolidated personal authority through four key institutional measures.

習近平主要透過四個重要制度措施來鞏固個人集權。

1 Promote organizational reform
推動組織改革

Reducing State Council departments and establishing new leading small groups and commission.

縮減國務院部門、創建新的領導小組與委員會。

2 Strictly enforcing disciplinary inspections
履行紀律檢查

Emphasizing political discipline and dispatching disciplinary inspection teams to party and government agencies.

強調政治紀律、向黨與政府機關派駐紀檢組。

4 Enhancing ideological education
強化思想教育

Inserting 'Xi Jinping Thought' into the Party Constitution and proposing the 'Two Upholds.'

通過「習近平思想」進入黨章、提出「兩個維護」。

Internally within the Party, Xi Jinping has established a historical position second only to Mao Zedong and Deng Xiaoping. He has served a third term as General Secretary of the Central Committee and State President, with his tenure as State President exceeding that of Mao Zedong.

在黨內樹立了僅次於毛澤東、鄧小平的歷史定位。目前，習近平擔任中共中央總書記、國家主席第三任期，其國家主席任期更超過毛澤東。

3 Revising party and state regulations
修改黨與國家規範

- Political Bureau members and Standing Committee members report to the Party Central Committee and the General Secretary.
- Amend the constitution to abolish the term limit for the President of China; incorporate "leadership of the Chinese Communist Party" and "Xi Jinping Thought" into the constitution.
- 政治局委員、常委向黨中央及總書記述職。
- 修憲取消國家主席任期制；將「中國共產黨領導」、「習思想」入憲。

The Party Central Committee has solidified its decision-making authority and leadership in various fields, gradually making the State Council an executing body of the Party.

黨中央鞏固各領域的決策權與主導地位，國務院逐漸成為黨的執行機關。

Institutional centralization: central leading small groups
制度化集權：中央工作領導小組

Promote organizational reform 推動組織改革

Reducing State Council departments and establishing new leading small groups and commission.
縮減國務院部門、創建新的領導小組與委員會。

Xi Jinping has implemented an important mechanism for institutionalizing the centralization of power by establishing new leading small groups.

習近平進行制度化集權的一個重要機制，就是建立許多新的領導小組。

The concept of leading small groups has appeared in the political history of the CCP before, notably during Mao Zedong's era in 1958, when he established five working groups covering areas such as politics and law, foreign affairs, and science.

領導小組的概念，在中共過去的政治史中並不是沒有出現過，最早是在毛澤東時期、1958 年的時候，當時毛澤東建立了五個工作小組，包括政法、外事、科學等。

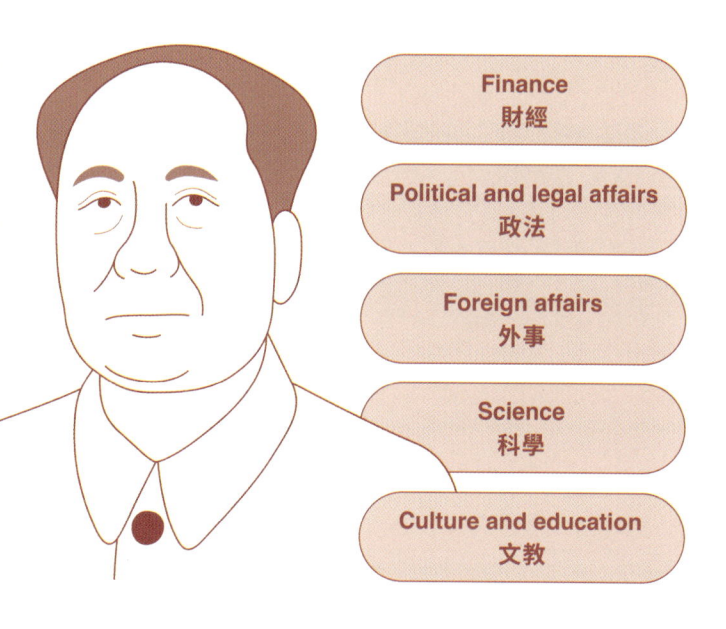

- Finance 財經
- Political and legal affairs 政法
- Foreign affairs 外事
- Science 科學
- Culture and education 文教

Typically, leading small groups serve as deliberative and coordinating bodies, operating as a form of "temporary working arrangement." However, under Xi Jinping, these leading small groups not only coordinate discussions but also directly decide on policies, effectively sidelining the power of the Politburo Standing Committee or the State Council.

領導小組一般是議事協調機構，屬於一種「臨時工作編制」。但是在習近平時期的工作領導小組，除了議事協調之外，也可以在裡面直接決定政策，這樣的模式，便直接架空了政治局常委，或者是國務院的權力。

Xi Jinping has also expanded and transformed some important leading small groups into commissions. Commissions are generally formalized and permanent institutions. While they still retain the concept of leading small groups, upgrading them to commissions allows for increased budgets and more staff to carry out policy work. This demonstrates Xi Jinping's emphasis on the leading small group model and his desire to strengthen governance under the Party's leadership through institutional upgrades, thereby consolidating his political authority further.

另外，習近平也把一些重要的領導小組，擴大改建成委員會，委員會一般是成建制的固定機構，雖然基本上委員會還是屬於領導小組的概念，但是升格為委員會後可以享有更多的預算、更多的幕僚人員來進行政策工作，因此它代表習近平十分重視領導小組的模式，並且希望透過升格的方式，加強以黨領政的措施，同時更加鞏固個人的政治權力。

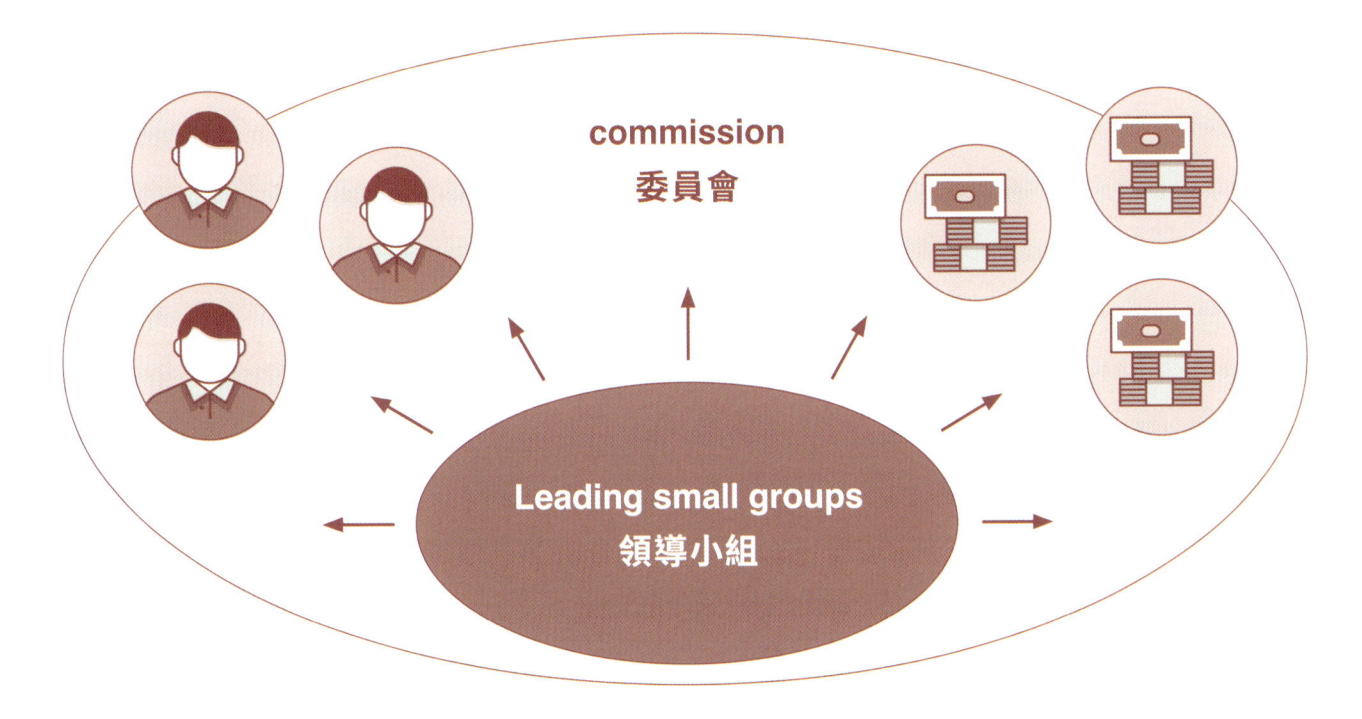

Institutionalized centralization: disciplinary inspection system
制度化集權：紀律檢查制度

2013

- Xi Jinping advocated for "fighting both tigers and flies together" in 2013.

- "Tigers" refer to high-ranking corrupt officials and "flies" refer to lower-level corrupt officials. This slogan essentially expanded the scope of anti-corruption efforts.

- 習近平提出老虎蒼蠅一起打。

- 老虎指的是大貪官，蒼蠅指的是比較基層的小貪官，老虎蒼蠅一起打，事實上就是擴大貪官整肅範圍。

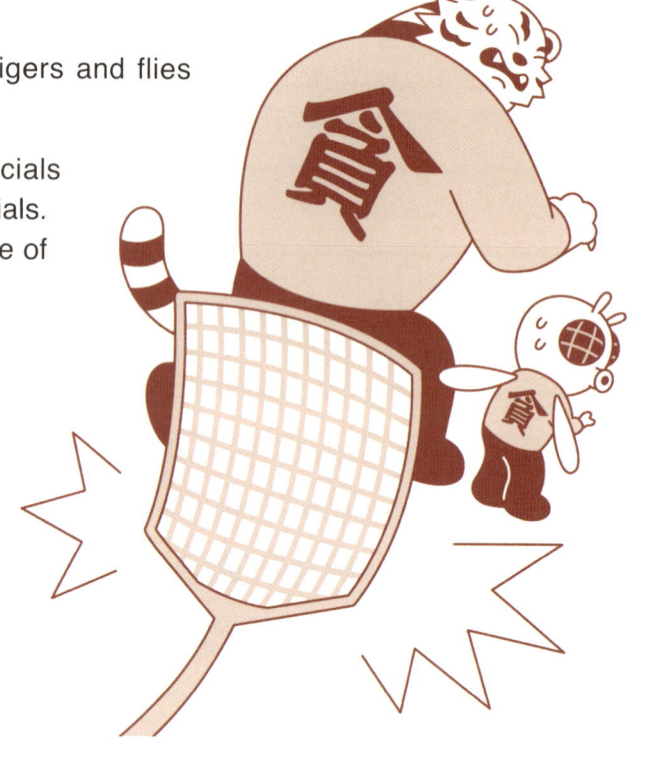

2015

- The Central Commission for Discipline Inspection dispatched discipline inspection teams to various Party departments such as the Organization Department, Propaganda Department, and government agencies including the State Council office.

- The Fifth Plenary Session passed the "Disciplinary Regulations," emphasizing political discipline and stipulating that criticism of central policies and deviation from Party and state guidelines would be subject to disciplinary investigation.

- This measure was largely aimed at intimidating officials into compliance with Xi Jinping's directives.

- 中紀委向黨部門中辦、中組、中宣等，政府部門國務院辦派駐紀檢組。

- 五中全會通過《紀律條例》，強調政治紀律，妄議中央、違背黨國家方針將受紀律調查。

- 很大程度是用來威懾官員，讓官員更能夠遵從習近平的旨意。

2017

Enforced strict discipline inspections
厲行紀律檢查

Emphasizing political discipline and dispatching disciplinary inspection teams to party and government agencies.

強調政治紀律、向黨與政府機關派駐紀檢組。

- The establishment of the National Supervisory Commission transformed the previous "double regulations" (where officials had to account for their actions at specified times and places) into a more formal, legally conceptualized "detention" for investigating problematic officials.

- "Detention" involves psychological intimidation through enclosed spaces and constant monitoring.

- Under this regime, trust is no longer placed in anyone, and officials have no personal sphere; their only option is to obey Xi Jinping's directives.

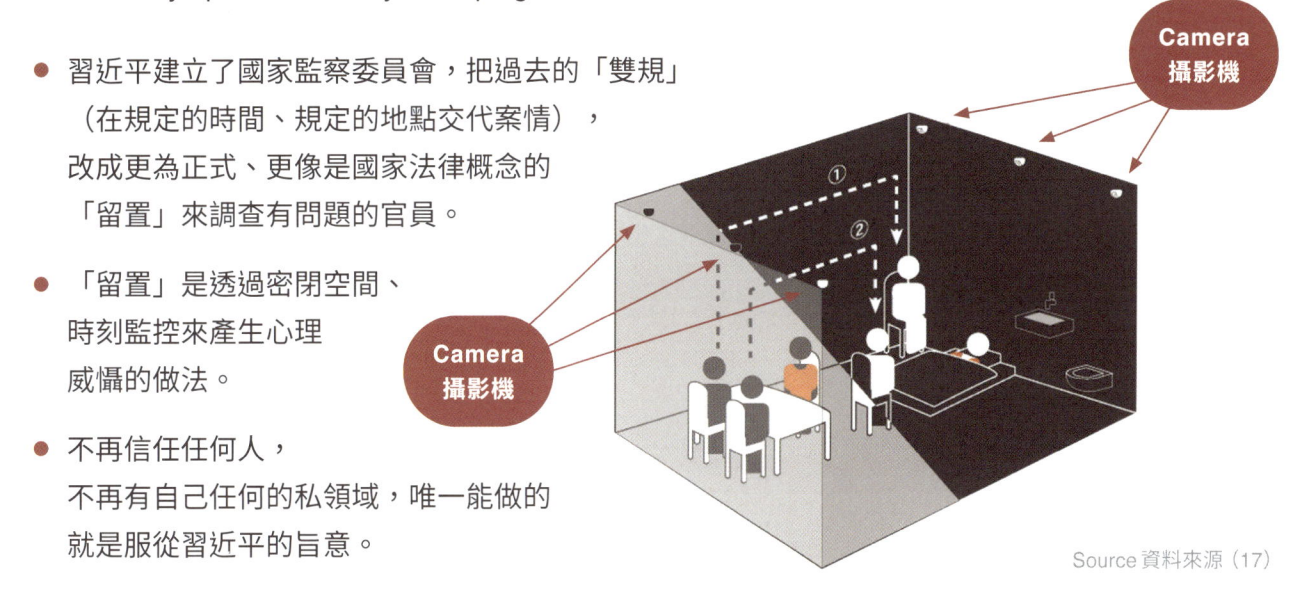

- 習近平建立了國家監察委員會，把過去的「雙規」（在規定的時間、規定的地點交代案情），改成更為正式、更像是國家法律概念的「留置」來調查有問題的官員。

- 「留置」是透過密閉空間、時刻監控來產生心理威懾的做法。

- 不再信任任何人，不再有自己任何的私領域，唯一能做的就是服從習近平的旨意。

Source 資料來源（17）

In addition to institutionalized centralization through leading small groups and disciplinary inspection systems, Xi Jinping has also employed a strategy of "campaign-style governance." This approach involves using official institutions, such as large-scale purges or mobilizations, to rally enthusiastic support for Xi Jinping among Party cadres and the public. While reminiscent of Mao Zedong's era, where similar campaign-style governance was prevalent, Xi Jinping's approach differs in that it combines these campaigns with institutional support, demonstrating a distinct form of centralized control compared to Mao's era.

而不管是在領導小組或紀律檢查制度的推行中，習近平在制度化集權之外，也採取了一種「運動型治理」的策略。所謂「運動型治理」，是指透過官方的制度，例如大規模的整肅或是動員，讓全黨的大幹部跟民眾掀起了一股擁護習近平的熱忱。這種情況跟毛澤東時期類似，但是如同前面所說，毛澤東時期只有「運動型治理」，但在習近平時期，除了運動型治理之外，同時還加上了制度層面的支撐，使得習近平所展現出來的集權模式，與毛澤東不同。

Chapter 2 | Through the red lens: an analysis of the CCP's political operations
紅色透視鏡：中共政治運作解析

Evolutionary milestones of dictators
獨裁者進化大事紀

2012

2017

First term (2012-2017)

2012
Elected as General Secretary of the Central Committee and Chairman of the Central Military Commission, beginning the first term.

2013
Elected as President of the People's Republic of China and Chairman of the National Military Commission, becoming the symbolic head of state representing the nation.

第一任期（2012年-2017年）

2012年
當選新一屆「中央委員會總書記」和「中央軍事委員會主席」，開始第一任期。

2013年
當選「中華人民共和國主席」和「國家軍委主席」，成為代表國家象徵的國家元首。

Second term (2017-2022)

2017
- At the 19th National Congress of the Chinese Communist Party, Xi Jinping was elected as a member of the 19th Central Committee. His ideology, "Xi Jinping Thought on Socialism with Chinese Characteristics for a New Era," was enshrined in the Party Constitution as the guiding ideology.
- At the first plenary session of the 19th Central Committee, Xi Jinping was re-elected as General Secretary of the Central Committee and Chairman of the Central Military Commission, starting his second term.
- The constitutional amendment removed the term limit for the State President and Vice President of the People's Republic of China, allowing them to serve more than two consecutive terms.

2018
Xi Jinping was re-elected as President of the People's Republic of China.

2022 — Now

第二任期（2017 年 -2022 年）

2017 年
- 中國共產黨第十九次全國代表大會上，習近平當選第十九屆中央委員，並通過將「習近平新時代中國特色社會主義思想」寫進《中國共產黨章程》，成為黨的指導思想

- 中共十九屆一中全會上，連任「中央委員會總書記」和「中央軍事委員會主席」，開始第二任期

- 通過憲法修正案，刪除國家主席、副主席「連續任職不得超過兩屆」的限制

2018 年
連任中華人民共和國主席

Third term (2022-present)

2022
At the First Plenary Session of the 20th Central Committee, Xi Jinping was re-elected as General Secretary of the Chinese Communist Party and Chairman of the Central Military Commission, marking the beginning of his third term.

2023
During the First Session of the 14th National People's Congress, Xi Jinping was re-elected as President of the People's Republic of China and Chairman of the National Military Commission. He became the first leader in the history of the People's Republic of China to serve more than three terms as President and to exceed 10 years in office as President.

第三任期（2022 年至今）

2022 年
二十屆一中全會上再次連任中共中央總書記和中共中央軍委主席，開始第三任期。

2023 年
十四屆全國人大一次會議連任國家主席和國家軍委主席，是中華人民共和國歷史上第一位國家主席任期超過三屆、主席任期超過 10 年的領導人。

2-3
The dilemma of dictators: succession crisis in the red empire
獨裁者的兩難：紅色帝國接班危機

Based on the above explanations, we can observe that under Xi Jinping's institutionalized centralization measures, both the state and Party systems in today's China have centralized power in his hands. This situation raises an important question: How will power be transitioned away from Xi Jinping in the later stages of his rule?

經由上述的說明，我們可以看到，現今的中國在習近平的制度化集權措施之下，國家系統與黨務系統的權力，皆集中在習近平手中。這樣的情形帶出了一個重要問題，也就是，在習近平統治的後期，會透過什麼方式將權力交接出去？

In authoritarian or non-democratic states, power transition is always a critical factor in determining stability. Unlike democratic systems where transitions can occur through stable and persuasive electoral processes involving various political parties, authoritarian regimes lack such mechanisms. Consequently, power transitions in authoritarian regimes often lead to political turbulence.

在威權體制，或者是非民主體制的國家當中，權力交接始終是主導國家是否可以穩定的關鍵。因為威權國家沒有辦法像民主體系的國家，可以透過選舉體制，以穩定、且對內部各政黨都具有說服力的方式選出下一屆領導人。因此威權體制國家的權力交接時常引起政局的動盪。

Furthermore, during power transitions in authoritarian systems, we must also consider the "dictator's dilemma." This dilemma arises because while dictators cultivate successors, they may become uneasy if the successor gains too much capability or popularity. This has been observed in historical examples like Mao Zedong and Deng Xiaoping, where successors arranged by Mao, such as Liu Shaoqi and Lin Biao, were eventually removed by Mao himself.

此外,在威權體制的權力交接過程,我們還要注意「獨裁者的兩難」,即是說獨裁者一方面會栽培接班人,但是如果接班人的能力或聲望太高,引起獨裁者的不安時,他可能會親自毀滅這個接班人,這從過去毛澤東、鄧小平的例子都可以看到,例如,劉少奇跟林彪是毛澤東安排的接班人,最後卻是由毛澤東親自剷除。

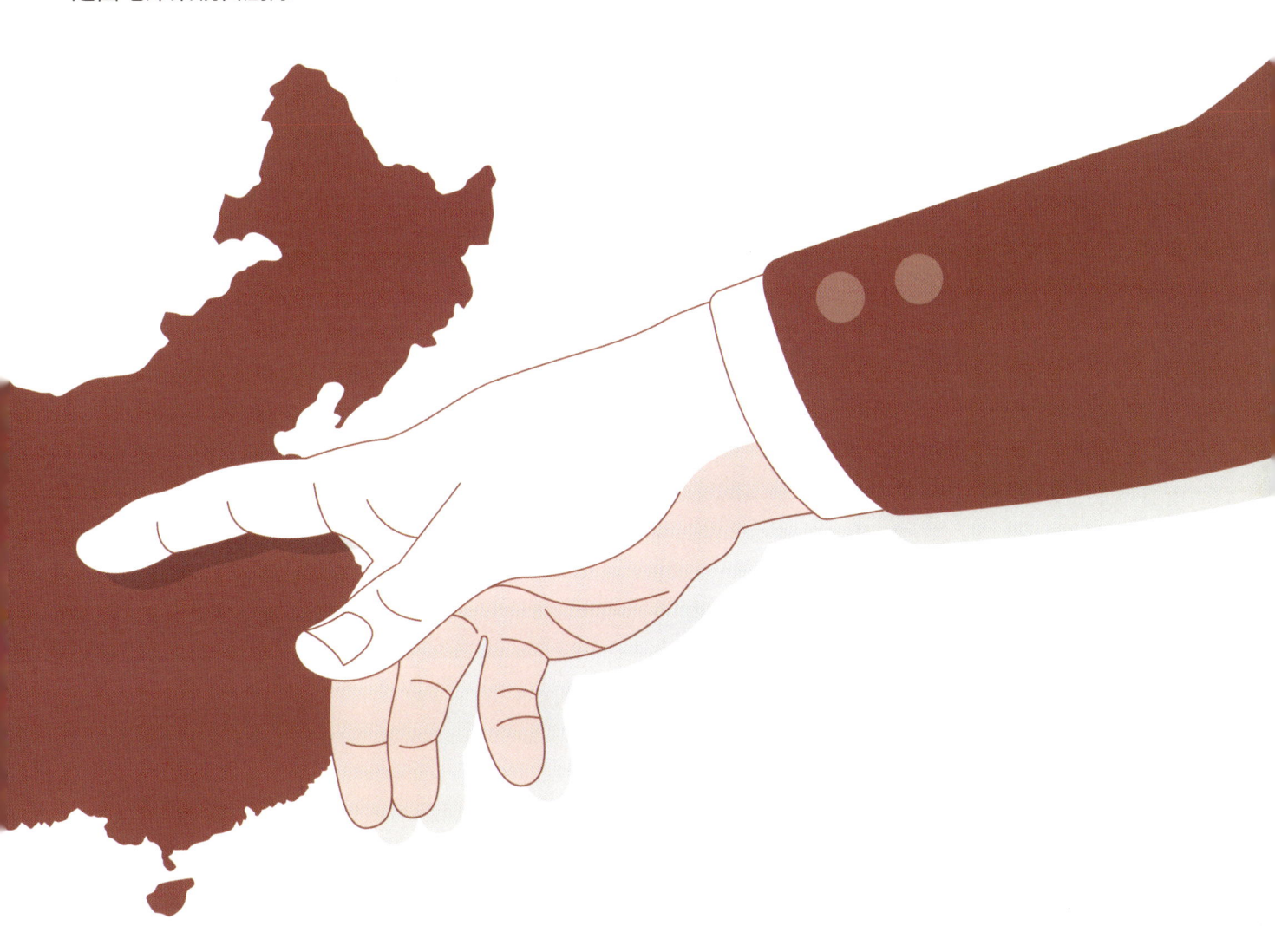

Therefore, whether the red empire can smoothly transition power and the dilemma faced by Xi Jinping as a dictator are crucial considerations when contemplating the issue of power transition during the Xi Jinping era.

因此,紅色帝國是否可以穩定的交接政權、以及目前習近平所面臨的獨裁者的兩難,是我們在思考後習近平時期權力交接問題時必須要注意的。

Power transition in the post-Xi era?
後習時代的權力交接

Given these similarities, the challenges Xi Jinping currently faces in power transition actually bear some resemblance to former Soviet General Secretary Brezhnev.

Firstly, Xi Jinping idolizes Mao Zedong, just as Brezhnev revered Stalin. Secondly, Xi Jinping has abolished economic reform measures introduced by his predecessors, mirroring Brezhnev's reversal of earlier economic reforms. Thirdly, Xi Jinping has allowed cadres to age gradually without promoting new officials, a trend also observed during Brezhnev's tenure.

Because of these parallels, when contemplating the power transition during the Xi era, we might draw lessons from Soviet history: After Brezhnev, the Soviet leadership aged significantly, economic stagnation ensued, and reforms only began with Gorbachev. However, Gorbachev, despite being young and less experienced, was not widely accepted by the Soviet party elite. These issues eventually led to the collapse of the Soviet Union. Given the current situation, there's a possibility that China in the future may experience similar challenges to the Soviet Union, leading to a certain degree of instability and collapse that we need to continue monitoring.

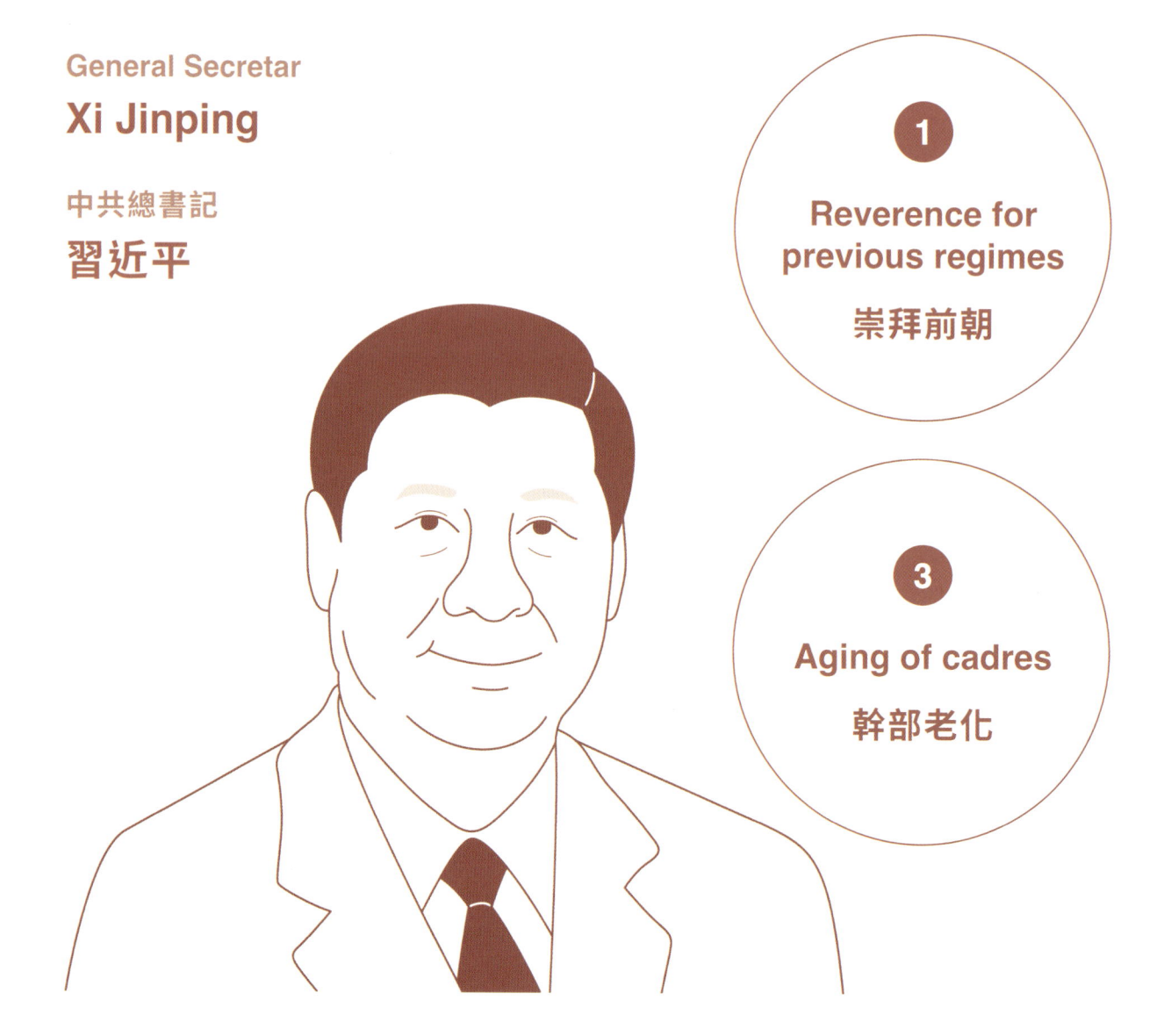

General Secretar
Xi Jinping

中共總書記
習近平

1
Reverence for previous regimes
崇拜前朝

3
Aging of cadres
幹部老化

習近平目前在權力交接上碰到的困境，其實跟蘇聯的前總書記布里茲涅夫有些類似。

第一，習近平崇拜毛澤東，而布里茲涅夫也崇拜前朝的史達林；第二，習近平廢除了前任領導人的經濟改革措施，而布里茲涅夫一樣也廢除了之前的經濟改革措施；第三，習近平開始讓幹部逐步老化、而不是提拔新幹部，而這個情形同樣也發生在布里茲涅夫時期。

因為這些相似性，我們在思考後習時期的權力交接時，也許可以借鑑蘇共的歷史：布里茲涅夫之後的蘇共，領導人高度老化、經濟嚴重的遲滯，要一直到戈巴契夫的時才開始改革，但是年輕的戈巴契夫資歷太淺，並不被蘇共的黨內人士所認同，種種問題最後造成了蘇共的瓦解跟崩潰。以目前的狀況而言，未來的中國很有可能會發生跟當時蘇共一樣的狀況，進而產生一定程度的不穩定與崩潰，這是我們需要持續留意的。

Former General Secretary of the Soviet Union

Breznev

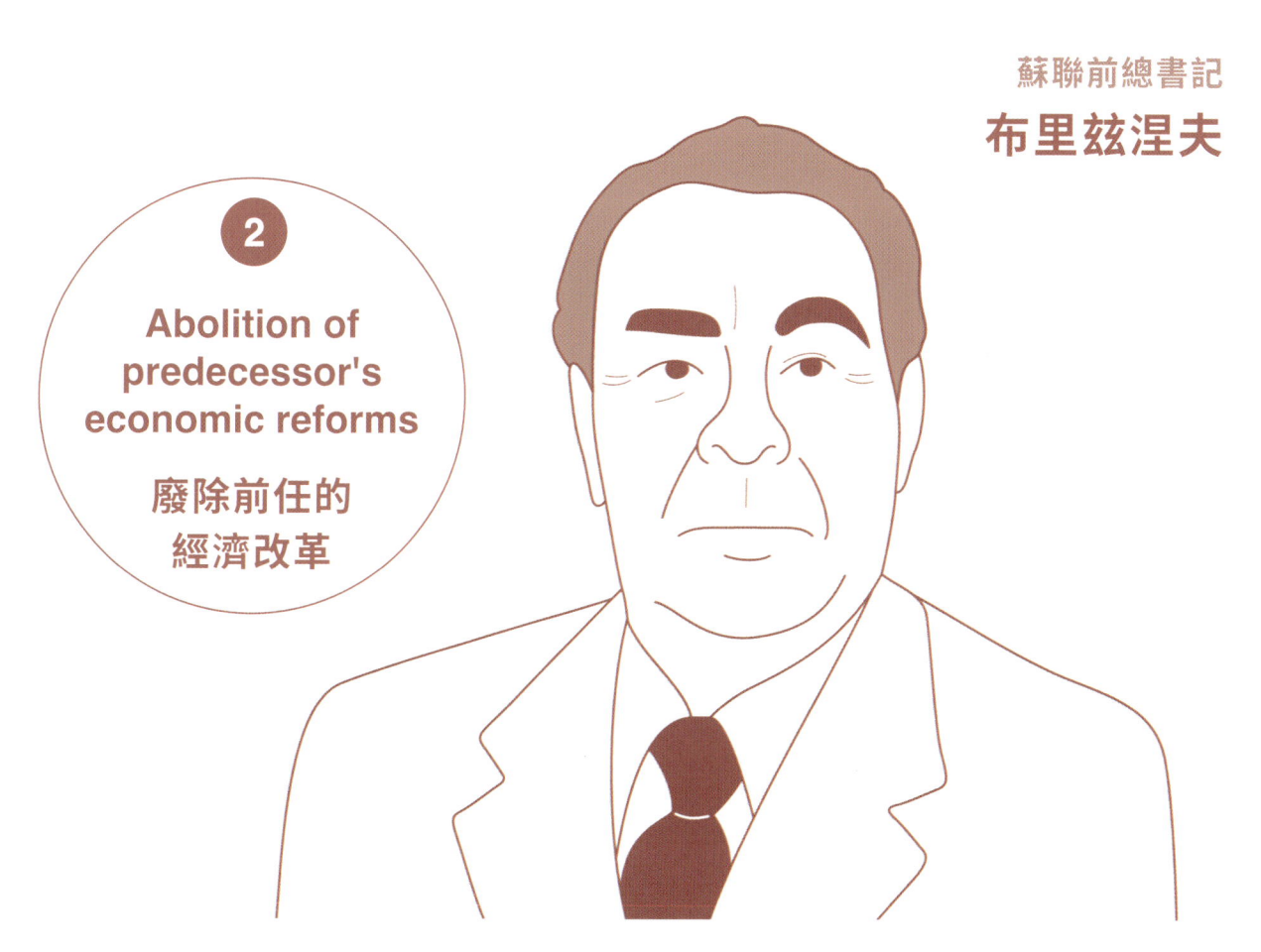

蘇聯前總書記

布里茲涅夫

2

Abolition of predecessor's economic reforms

廢除前任的經濟改革

67

Chapter 2 | Through the red lens: an analysis of the CCP's political operations
紅色透視鏡：中共政治運作解析

Healthy and safe
健康無虞

In addition to being re-elected for a third term as General Secretary, he will also seek re-election at the 21st Congress, meaning that the gradual transfer of power may not occur until the 22nd Congress in 2032.

In the second scenario, where Xi Jinping could gradually step down after 2032, the successor would likely be younger, possibly holding a position at the ministerial or deputy ministerial level. The successor would likely be male, as the CCP has not had any female Politburo Standing Committee members apart from Jiang Qing. Additionally, the successor would probably have a university degree, be of Han ethnicity, and have rotated through several departments, possibly coming from a technological bureaucratic background. Interestingly, none of the current visible members of the Xi faction are likely to ascend in this scenario.

他除了連任第三任總書記之外，在二十一大還會再連任一次，因此要一直到 2032 年的二十二大，才有可能把政權逐步交接出去。

而第二個情況，亦即習近平可以在 2032 年後逐步交棒的話，這個接班人的樣貌，基本上會是比較年輕、而且可能是在正部級或副部級的較年輕男性。因為中共除了江青之外，目前為止沒有其他女性有辦法進到政治局常委，接著一定是大專學歷、漢族，並可能在好幾個部門歷練、輪調過，可能是科技官僚。因此非常有趣的是，在第二種情況下，反而現在檯面上所看到的習家軍沒有一個會上位。

Young 年輕

Male 男性

Han People 漢族

None of the current visible members of the Xi faction are likely to ascend in this scenario.

反而現在檯面上習家軍沒有一個會上位

Not in good health before 2032
2032 前健康不佳

Currently, the most likely successor is one of the other six members of the Politburo Standing Committee. Among them, Li Qiang, Cai Qi, and Ding Xuexiang are the most probable candidates.

以目前來說，最有可能的接班人就是目前的其他六位政治局常委，而六人中相較更有可能的，會是李強、蔡奇跟丁薛祥這三人。

This raises an important question: Even if Xi Jinping arranges for a younger leader to take over after 2032, similar to Gorbachev in his time, will the current senior officials be willing to follow his lead? Will he be able to establish and maintain stability? If he initiates reforms akin to Gorbachev's, will these reforms succeed? Will they touch upon deep-seated party interests and create tensions within the central leadership? These are all issues that need to be carefully considered. During Xi Jinping's tenure as General Secretary, China will continue to consolidate power in a highly efficient manner, promote various constructions and policies, and generally maintain political stability. However, succession remains the biggest challenge facing the Red Empire in the later years of Xi Jinping's rule.

Li Qiang 李強
Cai Qi 蔡奇
Ding Xuexiang 丁薛祥
Wang Huning 王滬寧
Zhao Leji 趙樂際
Li Xi 李希

這便會碰到一個重要問題，即便習近平在 2032 年之後安排了一個年輕的領導人上來，就像當年的戈巴契夫上來一樣，那現在檯面上所見的這些舊臣，是不是願意聽他的話？這個人是不是能夠坐得穩、坐得住？這個人如果像戈巴契夫一樣推出相關改革，這些改革能否成功？是否會觸動黨內的深層利益、造成中南海內部的緊張局勢？這都是台灣人民需要關注的狀況。

在習近平接任總書記的這幾年當中，中國會持續以一個高度有效率的方式來強化集權，進行各種建設以及各方面政策的推動，在政治上大致上也會是穩定的，但是因為上述種種情形，接班問題，會是紅色帝國在習近平後期面臨的最大困難。

社會科學類　PF0365

解密中國：習近平統治下的共產黨與解放軍
Real China: The Communist Party and the People's Liberation Army under Xi Jinping

編　　著 / 財團法人中央廣播電臺
統籌策畫 / 財團法人中央廣播電臺
　　　　　104 臺北市中山區北安路55號
　　　　　電話：+886-2-2885-6168
　　　　　https://www.rti.org.tw/
出版統籌 / 賴秀如Cheryl Lai
總 策 畫 / 張瑞昌Chang Jui-Chang
副總策畫 / 沈聰榮Shen Tsung-jung、李冠毅Lee Kuan-yi、李明俐Isis Mingli Lee、
　　　　　林啟驊Chihua Lin、陳德愉Chen De-yu
編輯小組 / 沈宜芬Anne Shen、周秀梅Marian Chou、陳錦榮Chen Jing-rong、
　　　　　曾偉旻Tseng Wei-min、黃美寧Huang Mei-ning、黃佳山Carlson Huang、
　　　　　楊嘉慧Yang Chia-hui、詹逸文Chan Yi-wen（依姓氏筆畫排列）
執行製作 / 央廣學院Rti Academy
責任編輯 / 王聖芬Salome Sheng-Fen Wang
華語編輯與校對 / Hahow 好學校
英語編輯與校對 / CLN (Corporate Language Network)
插畫與美術設計 / Hahow 好學校
發 行 人 / 宋政坤
法律顧問 / 毛國樑　律師
印製出版 / 秀威資訊科技股份有限公司
　　　　　114台北市內湖區瑞光路76巷65號1樓
　　　　　電話：+886-2-2796-3638　傳真：+886-2-2796-1377
　　　　　http://www.showwe.com.tw
劃撥帳號 / 19563868　戶名：秀威資訊科技股份有限公司
　　　　　讀者服務信箱：service@showwe.com.tw
展售門市 / 國家書店（松江門市）
　　　　　104台北市中山區松江路209號1樓
　　　　　電話：+886-2-2518-0207　傳真：+886-2-2518-0778
網路訂購 / 秀威網路書店：http://www.bodbooks.com.tw
　　　　　國家網路書店：http://www.govbooks.com.tw

2025年2月　BOD一版
定價：450元
版權所有　翻印必究
本書如有缺頁、破損或裝訂錯誤，請寄回更換

國家圖書館出版品預行編目（CIP）資料

解密中國：習近平統治下的共產黨與解放軍 = Real China : the Communist Party and the People's Liberation Army under Xi Jinping / 財團法人中央廣播電臺編著. -- 一版. -- 臺北市：秀威資訊科技股份有限公司, 2025.02
　　面；　公分. -- (社會科學類)
BOD 版
ISBN 978-626-7511-59-6(平裝)

1. CST: 習近平　2. CST: 政治制度　3. CST: 兩岸關係
4. CST: 中國大陸研究

574.1　　　　　　　　　　　　　　　114000203

Copyright©2025 by Showwe Information Co., Ltd.
Printed in Taiwan
All Rights Reserved

讀者回函卡

Acknowledgements
致謝

Radio Taiwan International (Rti), as a national broadcaster with expertise in international communication and multilingual proficiency, is honored to present "Real China: The Communist Party and the People's Liberation Army under Xi Jinping" to our beloved Taiwan.

"Real China: The Communist Party and the People's Liberation Army under Xi Jinping" is a bilingual manual. From its conceptualization, content development, and course planning, to Chinese text writing, English translation, illustration, layout editing, design, and printing, both in form and content, this manual is a result of the collective wisdom and efforts of many people.

First, we would like to thank the National Development Council and the Bilingual Policy Office of the Executive Yuan for their funding, which allowed us to develop the content. We also appreciate the Ministry of Culture, as Rti's supervisory authority, for consistently recognizing Rti's expertise in multilingual and international communication. We extend our thanks to the Taiwan Association for Strategic Simulation (TASS), a team composed of former national security personnel, responsible for the content development of this book and who also serve as Rti's professional consultants in the national security research. Additionally, we thank our instructors who collaborated with Rti: Tsai Wen-Hsuan (Researcher, the Institute of Political Science, Academia Sinica), Huang Jaw-Nian (Associate Professor, the Graduate Institute of Development Studies, National Chengchi University), Josh Wang (Co-host of the Taiwan Information Environment Research Center), and Guo Li-Sheng (Retired Major General of the Republic of China Army). Their extensive knowledge, experience, and research contributions have endowed this manual with a strong and vibrant soul.

In addition to thanking the Rti Board of Directors and all department heads and colleagues for their full support, we also extend our gratitude to Hahow for their efforts in illustration and editing, and CLN for their professional English translation. Without you, the bilingual manual "Real China: The Communist Party and the People's Liberation Army under Xi Jinping" would not have been possible.

"Real China: The Communist Party and the People's Liberation Army under Xi Jinping" is a collective work of wisdom. We hope that while you read this manual and learn about China, you will feel Rti's dedication and mission, gain knowledge and strength, and join us in contributing to Taiwan's democratic resilience.

中央廣播電臺（Radio Taiwan International，Rti）做為兼具國際傳播與多語專業的國家廣播媒體，非常榮幸地把《解密中國：習近平統治下的共產黨與解放軍》，獻給我們摯愛的臺灣。

《解密中國：習近平統治下的共產黨與解放軍》是一本雙語手冊，從概念的發想孵育、內容研發與課程規劃、華語文字撰稿、英語翻譯、插畫繪製、圖文落版編輯、設計到印刷出版，無論是形式還是內容，都匯聚了眾人的智慧心血結晶。

首先要感謝行政院國家發展委員會以及雙語政策辦公室的補助，讓我們有經費進行內容研發；感謝文化部，作為央廣的主管機關，一直對央廣的多語與國際傳播專業表示認同。也謝謝台灣戰略模擬學會，他們是一群由前國安人員所組成的團隊，負責本書的內容研發，也擔任央廣的國安研究領域專業顧問。還有與央廣合作的四位講師：蔡文軒（中研院政治所研究員）、黃兆年（政大國發所副教授）、王希（台灣資訊環境研究中心共同主持人）、郭力升（中華民國陸軍備役少將），是他們以豐沛的知識、經驗與研究成果，賦予這本手冊強韌的靈魂。

除了感謝央廣董事會和各部門主管、同仁全力協助之外，我們也要感謝 Hahow 好學校在繪製與編輯的努力、CLN 的英語翻譯專業，沒有你們，這本《解密中國：習近平統治下的共產黨與解放軍》雙語手冊就無法順利面世。

《解密中國：習近平統治下的共產黨與解放軍》是眾人的智慧結晶。希望大家在閱讀本手冊、認識中國的同時，能感受到央廣的用心與使命，也得到知識與力量，共同為台灣的民主韌性盡一份心力。

Source
資料來源

(1) David Shambaugh, "China's Long March to Global Power."

(2) Wu Jieh-Min, "Mechanisms of Influence and Resistance in the 'China Factor,'" Anaconda in the Chandelier: Mechanisms of Influence and Resistance in the "China Factor," pp. 35-36.
吳介民,《吊燈裡的巨蟒》, P.35-36,〈中國因素作用力與反作用力〉。

(3) Interview with Professor Huang Jaw-Nian; graph made by TASS.
黃兆年教授訪談,TASS 製圖。

(4) Interview with Professor Huang Jaw-Nian; graph made by TASS.
黃兆年教授訪談,TASS 製圖。

(5) HUANG Jaw-Nian, 2023, "China's Propaganda and Disinformation Operations in Taiwan."

(6) Interview with Professor Huang Jaw-Nian; graph made by TASS.
黃兆年教授訪談,TASS 製圖。

(7) HUANG Jaw-Nian, 2023, "China's Propaganda and Disinformation Operations in Taiwan."

(8) Historical annual reports of Want Want China Holdings; Huang Jaw-Nian, 2022, "The China Factor, Dual Government-Business Relations, and Taiwanese Media's Self-Censorship," pp. 10-11.
中國旺旺歷年財報;黃兆年,2022,〈中國因素、雙重政商關係與臺灣媒體自我審查〉, P.10-11。

(9) Newtalk.tw, Lin Chau-Yi, "Marketing Fujian Province On ChinaTimes; Chinese officials: We will wire money to ChinaTimes once we receive the invoice," 2012/03/30.
Newtalk 新聞,林朝億,〈福建置入中時 陸官員:發票來了 錢就匯過去〉2012.03.30。

(10) Historical surveys on the TV and film industry conducted by Taiwan Institute of Economic Research; Huang Jaw-Nian, 2022, "The China Factor, Dual Government-Business Relations, and Taiwanese Media's Self-Censorship," pp. 10-11.
台灣經濟研究院歷年影視產業調查報告;黃兆年,2022,〈中國因素、雙重政商關係與臺灣媒體自我審查〉, P.10-11。

(11) Taiwan News Smart Web; Huang Jaw-Nian, 2022, "The China Factor, Dual Government-Business Relations, and Taiwanese Media's Self-Censorship," pp. 10-11.
台灣新聞智慧網;黃兆年,2022,〈中國因素、雙重政商關係與臺灣媒體自我審查〉, P.10-11。

(12) Interview with IORG's co-director Josh Wang. Diagram by TASS.
訪談 IORG 共同主持人王希,TASS 製圖。

(13) Interview with IORG's co-director Josh Wang. Diagram by TASS.
訪談 IORG 共同主持人王希,TASS 製圖。

(14) IORG 2022 DA 28.

(15) IORG Message Credibility Assessment I Current Event Exercise No. 9.
IORG 訊息可信度評量,時事練習題,第 9 題。

(16) IORG 2022 DA 37.

(17) Researcher Tsai Wen-hsuan from the Institute of Political Science at Academia Sinica.
中研院政治所蔡文軒研究員

(18) Academia Historica.
國史館。

(19) Marine Geology.

(20) earth.nullschool.

(21) Wind power information integration platform.
風力資訊整合平台。

The future development of PLA military operations
解放軍軍事行動的未來發展

Based on various information accumulated from the IPB, we can reasonably predict the PLA's military actions:

1 — Reduced feasibility of traditional joint amphibious landing operations
Joint amphibious landings are faced with daunting challenges and great risk related to a range of factors: sea conditions, climate, terrain, and temporal-spatial constraints on the Taiwan Strait battlefield.

2 — The PLA's military development
Large transport aircraft and helicopters are mass-produced and the number of these aircraft in PLA's possession is gradually rising. In the future, the feasibility of conducting air-landing operations to seize ports and airborne landing to seize airports will gradually increase.

3 — Adjusting Taiwan's future defense strategies
The northern part of Taiwan where Taipei Port, Taoyuan Airport, and Songshan Airport are located, is the most important area. The ROC Armed Forces should continue to improve its anti-airborne and anti-special attack capabilities.

4 — In the future, PLA military drills may still turn into actual military attacks.
The PLA has large-scale movements by increasing war reserves and requisitioning civilian resources. These actions are difficult to escape modern battlefield surveillance. Therefore, if China were to attack Taiwan by "transition from exercises to combat," the environment of the battlefield in Taiwan and the international situation would have to be considered. We must first strengthen ourselves before we can resist the PLA's attack with the resilience of the entire society.

綜合戰場情報準備所累積的種種資訊，我們來預測未來中國對台軍事可能行動：

1 — 傳統兩棲可行性降低
聯合兩棲登陸難度大、風險高，受台海戰場環境的海象、氣候、地形、時間與空間等因素限制。

2 — 解放軍建軍發展
大型運輸機、直升機都已經量產且數量逐步增加，未來機降奪港口、空降奪機場，可能性已經越來越高。

3 — 未來台灣的防守構想調整
台灣的北部，包括台北港、桃園機場、松山機場為重中之重，國軍應持續精進「反空降」、「反特攻」的能力。

4 — 解放軍未來仍可能透過由演轉戰攻台
共軍大規模兵力調動、增加戰爭儲備、徵用民間資源等行動，皆難逃現代戰場情監偵的法眼，不易隱匿其企圖。故未來若是以「由演轉戰」模式攻臺，仍要考量臺灣戰場環境特徵與國際局勢。臺灣必須先強備自身，才能以全社會防衛韌性，抵擋中共解放軍的攻臺行動。

Real China: The Communist Party and the People's Liberation Army under Xi Jinping
解密中國：習近平統治下的共產黨與解放軍

3-4
Maritime or airborne warfare: How will the PLA initiate the war?
海上來還是天上來：解放軍怎麼打？

Military operation stage
- Transitioning from military exercises to military operations.
- The deployment of amphibious and airborne operational forces is estimated to be no less than 55,000 troops.

Potential challenges
- The regular transport capacity of the PLA mainly involves amphibious forces and airlifting and airborne forces. For now, we assess that their regular transport capacity is insufficient to support large-scale military operations. They may incorporate civilian transport capacity into their regular transport capacity.
- Civilian transportation cannot be used to seize beachheads. Its sole use is after ports are secured, to assist with administrative unloading.

The key to force projection
- Airports and ports are critical to the PLA's large-scale force projection. Once airports and ports fall under the PLA's control, the PLA combat strength would increase, marking a turning point in the balance of forces between us and the enemy.
- Therefore, the best time for us to go into battle is before the PLA establishes landing sites.

軍事發起
- 由軍演轉變軍事行動。
- 預估首波投入的兩棲與空降作戰部隊兵力不少於 5.5 萬人。

可能面臨問題
- 中共常規部隊的運輸能量，主要是由兩棲運輸部隊跟空機降的運輸部隊支援，目前研判常規的運能是不足以支持大規模的軍事行動，可能額外徵用民用運輸能量。
- 民用運輸能量無法搶灘登陸，唯有在奪取港口、開放之後才能支援行政下卸。

兵力投射關鍵
- 機場與港口是解放軍大量兵力投射的關鍵，當機場、港口遭到解放軍控領開放時，就是解放軍增長戰力的關鍵時刻，也可能是敵我戰力消長的轉折點。
- 因此我軍的作戰最佳時期，即是在解放軍建立登陸場前。

PLA personnel and system
人員組成與制度

Personnel 人力組成

- 2 million active personnel, lmaybe the largest armed force in the world in terms of scale.
- There are about 450,000 officers and civilian personnel and about 850,000 non-commissioned officers.
- About 700,000 conscripts.

- 現役人員 200 萬人
- 軍官與文職人員約 45 萬人、士官約 85 萬人
- 義務役約 70 萬人

Conscription 徵兵制度

- There are approximately 400,000 recruits every year through enlistment and conscription.
- The military service lasts 2 years, after which, one can retire, be selected as a non-commissioned officer, or enter the military academy to be promoted to a commissioned officer.
- In 2020, compulsory military service was adjusted to hold a two-phase conscription cycle per year with the first cycle starting in March and the second in September.

- 每年新兵約 40 萬名（自願或義務參軍）
- 役期 2 年，役滿可選擇退伍、被選為士官，或進入軍事學院升為軍官
- 2020 年調整為 2 徵 2 退，入伍時間為 3 月和 9 月

Chapter 3 | Dismantle the PLA's attack plans for Taiwan: PLA's military operations against Taiwan
破解解放軍攻臺策略：共軍對臺軍事行動

Five major services
五大軍種

Ground force 陸軍	Mobile Warfare Forces, Border and Coastal Defense Forces, Garrison (Hong Kong, Macau) 機動作戰部隊、邊境和海岸防禦部隊、駐紮部隊（香港、澳門）
Navy 海軍	Submarine Force, Surface Vessel Force, Marine Corps, Naval Air Force, Coastal Defense Force 潛艦部隊、水面艦部隊、海軍陸戰隊、航空部隊、岸防部隊
Air force 空軍	Air Force, Airborne Forces, Surface-to-air Missile Force, Radar force, Electronic Countermeasure Forces, Communications Force 航空部隊、空降部隊、地對空導彈部隊、雷達部隊、電子對抗部隊、通訊部隊
Rocket force 火箭軍	Submarine Force, Surface Vessel Force, Marine Corps, Naval Air Force, Coastal Defense Force 潛艦部隊、水面艦部隊、海軍陸戰隊、航空部隊、岸防部隊
Strategic support force 戰略支援部隊	Support troops for battlefield environment, information, communications, information security, and new technology testing 戰場環境、資訊、通訊、資安、新科技測試的支援部隊

downgrade and restructure into
降級拆分成

Reorganization announced on 2024/4/19 宣佈改制	(Information communication base) 信息通信基地	(Formerly the network systems department) 原網路系統部	(Formerly the space systems department) 原航天系統部
Strategic support force 戰略支援部隊 →	**Information support force** 信息支援部隊 +	**Cyberspace force** 網路空間部隊 +	**Military aerospace force** 軍事航天部隊

Arms
兵種

Joint logistics support force 聯勤保障部隊	Support forces for inventories and warehousing, medical services, transportation, force projection, petroleum pipelines, engineering and construction management, reserve asset management, procurement 庫存和倉儲、醫療服務、運輸、部隊投射、石油管道、工程和建築管理、儲備資產管理、採購的支援部隊

From five major military services to four major military services
從五大軍種到「四大軍種、四大兵種」

The five military services are the Ground Force, Navy, Air Force, Rocket Force, and Strategic Support Force, each with their own operating forces. Additionally, there are troops directly commanded by the CMC, namely, the Joint Logistics Support Force and the People's Armed Police Force.

In late April 2024, the CMC launched a new wave of organizational restructuring mainly by downgrading and splitting up the formerly "military branch-level" Strategic Support Force into the "arms-level" forces: Information Support Force, Cyberspace Force, and Military Aerospace Force. Since the Information Support Force had been established in late April, the creation of the other two forces is therefore worth anticipating shortly.

The purpose of this restructuring is twofold. Firstly, it has re-divided the "Strategic Support Force," which was formerly composed of three different forces, based upon functional and professional considerations. This restructuring helps to improve efficiency in organizational development, personnel management, equipment utilization, and budget allocation. The second purpose is aimed to appoint two more generals to lead the two newly established forces. Xi Jinping would leverage his strength as a leader by the addition of two more army generals.

五大軍種，亦即陸軍，海軍，空軍，火箭軍，以及戰略支援部隊。各軍種下有不同的作戰部隊。至於軍委直屬的部隊，主要有聯勤保障部隊，以及人民武裝部隊。

到了2024年4月下旬，中共展開另一波的組織調整方案。這個方案最主要的內容，就是把原來的戰略支援部隊，降級、拆分開來，分別是原本屬於「軍種級」的戰略支援部隊，變成屬於「兵種級」的「信息支援部隊」、「網路空間部隊」以及「軍事航天部隊」。其中信息支援部隊已經在4月下旬先行成立，未來可以持續注意，是否會先後再成立網路空間部隊跟軍事太空部隊。

這一波組織的調整有兩個重點。第一，它將原本由三個不同部隊組成的「戰略支援部隊」，以職能化、專業化的角度重新再分拆開來，可以讓部隊組織發展、人員經管、裝備運用、預算調撥等都更有效率。第二，新增部隊可能皆由上將級軍事首長領導，因此未來可能增加兩席上將位置供習近平運用，增加他的人事運用籌碼。

| Ground force 陸軍 | Navy 海軍 | Air force 空軍 | Rocket force 火箭軍 | Strategic support force 戰略支援部隊 |

The five theater commands evolved from the five military regions, which were formerly six military regions, eleven military regions, and seven military regions at different points in history. The current five theater commands were established after military reforms in 2017 and 2018. Whether it be theater commands or military regions, they have undergone changes of regional deployments since the Chinese Civil War.

五大戰區的前身是五大軍區，而五大軍區的前身，曾經有六大軍區、十一大軍區、七大軍區等等，最後在 2017、2018 年的軍改之後，變成現在的五大戰區。不管是現在的戰區或是以前的軍區，其實都是當年國共內戰之後，共軍分區配置部署，逐漸演化到現在的狀況。

Five Theater Commands
五大戰區

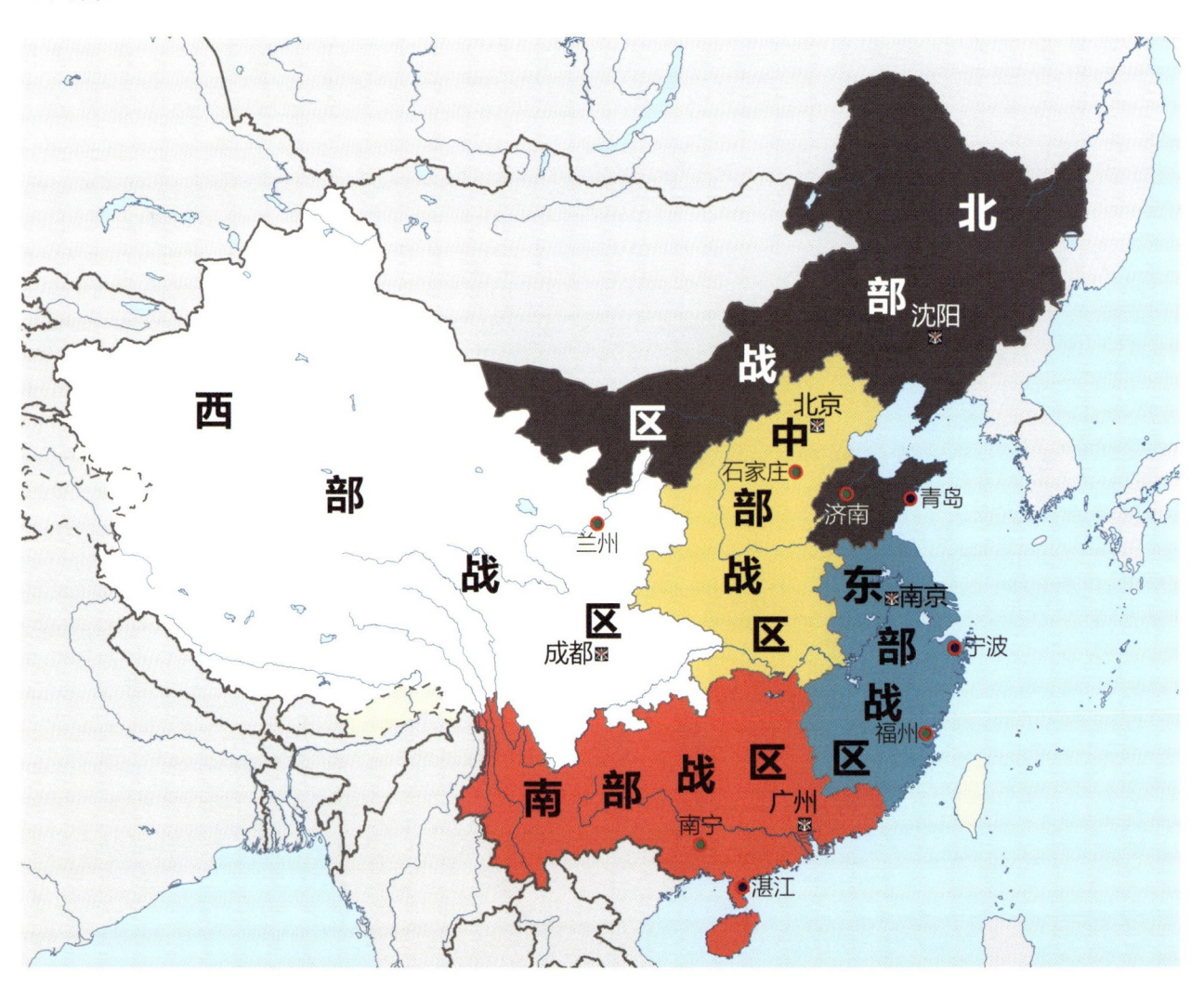

Real China: The Communist Party and the People's Liberation Army under Xi Jinping
解密中國：習近平統治下的共產黨與解放軍

Chairman of the CMC
Xi Jinping
President of the country

軍委主席
習近平
國家主席

↓ Conducts commands
　 指揮

Vice chairman of the CMC
Zhang Youxia
General

軍委副主席
張又俠
陸軍上將

Vice chairman of the CMC
He Weidong
General

軍委副主席
何衛東
陸軍上將

Member of the CMC
Miao Hua
Director of the political work department
Admiral

軍委成員
苗華
政工主任
海軍上將

Member of the CMC
Zhang Shengmin
Secretary of the CMC discipline inspection commission
General of the rocket force

軍委成員
張升民
紀委書記
火箭軍上將

Joint staff department 聯合參謀部	Political work department 政治工作部	Commission for discipline inspection 紀檢委員會
Combat training 作戰訓練工作	Ideological education and party group establishment 思想教育與黨組建設	Disciplinary review 紀律審查
Commander, deputy commander 司令員、副司令員	Political commissar, deputy political commissar 政委、副政委	Leader of discipline inspection team 紀檢組組長

85

LA's military structure and five theater commands
中央軍委會與五大戰區

The Central Military Commission (CMC) heads the People's Liberation Army of China. Xi Jinping serves as Chair of the CMC, with two vice-chairmen and four members. The four members of the CMC are: the Minister of Defense, Chief of the Joint Staff Department, who serves as Staff Commissioner, Director of the Political Work Department, who serves as Political Commissioner, and Secretary of the CMC Discipline Inspection Commission, who serves as Discipline Commissioner. Xi Jinping utilizes the three key pillars: Joint Staff, Political Work, and Discipline Inspection, to exert control over the party's ideology, construction, and discipline. This arrangement illustrates that the PLA is an organization that abides by the principle of the party's leadership over the military.

中央軍委會是中共解放軍最高指揮單位。我們在第一單元中提到，中央軍委主席是由習近平擔任，另有兩位副主席與四位軍委委員。在四位委員中，除國防部長之外，分別由聯合參謀部的參謀長來擔任參謀委員，由政治工作部的主任來擔任政治委員，由紀律檢察委員會的書記擔任紀律委員。習近平藉由「參、政、紀」這三個職能，來嚴管他的思想、黨的建設還有紀律審查，可以從這邊看到，中國解放軍是徹底貫治以黨領軍理念的一個組織。

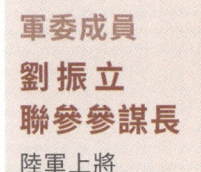

Member of the CMC
Dong Jun
Minister of national defense
Admiral

軍委成員
董軍｜國防部長
海軍上將

Member of the CMC
Liu Zhenli
Chief of the joint staff department
General

軍委成員
劉振立
聯參參謀長
陸軍上將

Department 部門

Main operations 主管業務

Theater commands 戰區

Real China: The Communist Party and the People's Liberation Army under Xi Jinping
解密中國：習近平統治下的共產黨與解放軍

Central military commission　中央軍委

7 Departments(Offices)　7個部（廳）

- General office
  辦公廳
- Joint staff department
  聯合參謀部
- Political work department
  政治工作部
- Logistics support department
  後勤保障部
- Equipment development department
  裝備發展部
- National defense mobilization department
  國防動員部
- Training and administration department
  訓練管理部

3 Commissions　3個委員會

- Discipline inspection commission
  紀律檢查委員會
- Politics and law commission
  政法委員會
- Science and technology commission
  科學基數委員會

5 Directly affiliated bodies　5個直屬機構

- Office for reform and organizational structure
  改革和編制辦公室
- Office for international military cooperation
  國際軍事合作辦公室
- Office for strategic planning
  戰略規劃辦公室
- Audit office
  審計署
- Agency for offices administration
  機關事務管理總局

Services　軍種

- Ground force 陸軍
- Navy 海軍
- Air force 空軍
- Rocket force 火箭軍
- Strategic support force 戰略支援部隊

Theater commands　戰區

- Eastern theater command 東部戰區
- Southern theater command 南部戰區
- Western theater command 西部戰區
- Northern theater command 北部戰區
- Central theater command 中部戰區

Troops　部隊

這裡提供的範例具時效性內容

3-3
The ground force, navy, air force + PLA's rocket force: introduction to the PLA
陸海空 + 火箭軍：解放軍軍隊介紹

PLA command system
中共解放軍指揮體系

Since we've gained a solid grasp of the geographical factors of Taiwan's tactical environment and their impact on our military actions, we will proceed to discuss the third step of the IPB: assessing the enemy's threat. In this step, we will look into the composition of the PLA.

First, let's take a look at the command system of the People's Liberation Army of China. We will give an account of the three major parts of the command system:

1 The Central Military Commission (CMC) Exercises Overall Leadership: The CMC leads the theater commands and military services, tackling warfare preparations and developing military services. It is the highest command unit.

2 The Theater Commands Take Charge of Military Operations: Currently, there are five theater commands: Central, Southern, Western, Northern, and Eastern theater commands, responsible for specific warfare preparations and military operations.

3 The Military Services Focus on Development: There are five military services in China: the Ground Force, Navy, Air Force, Rocket Force, and Strategic Support Force. These forces are in charge of building combat capabilities, executing training, and equipping and supplying troops before they are taken over and commanded by the theater commands in military operations.

充分了解了台灣作戰環境的地理因素以及其對相關軍事行動的影響之後，接下來我們要進行到，戰場情報準備的第三步驟，敵軍威脅評估，那麼在這個步驟裡面，我們要來認識中共解放軍的組成。

首先我們先來看中國人民解放軍的指揮體系，在指揮體系中，我們用三部分來說明：

1 軍委管「總」：中央軍委負責指導戰區跟軍種，分別推動備戰任務以及軍種的建設，是最高指揮單位。

2 戰區主「戰」：目前中共編制有，中、南、西、北、東五大戰區，負責特定的備戰以及軍事作戰任務。

3 軍種主「建」：中共有「陸」、「海」、「空」、「火箭軍」以及「戰略支援部隊」五大軍種，負責建置軍種的部隊戰力，並執行訓練、裝備籌補等任務，之後交由戰區來指揮執行作戰任務。

Impact of Taiwan's environment on island landing operations
台灣環境對登島行動之影響

Building on the previous discussions, we have compiled the impact and constraints of Taiwan's environment on amphibious landing operations. Faced with frequent military threats from China, we can use a table to assess the PLA's potential for joint amphibious operations, bolstering our confidence in robust self-defense measures.

綜合前面的內容，我們整理了台灣環境對於兩棲登島行動的影響與限制。面對中國頻繁的武力威脅，我們可以用表格檢查解放軍聯合兩棲登島的可能性，強韌自我防衛的信心。

Supply loading and ferrying 裝載與航渡	Joint-landing operation 聯合登陸	Land warfare 陸上作戰
Seasonal wind direction affects departure location and navigation conditions. For example, departing from Sandu Ao Military Port in summer would be sailing against the wind. In winter, departing from Chaoshan would be sailing upwind. 季節風向影響發航地與航行條件，如夏季由三都澳基地發航，將逆風航行。冬天從潮汕發航，亦面臨逆風航行。	**Amphibious landing 兩棲登陸** - Limited landing locations. - If the troops are obstructed by buildings after landing, there would be limited opportunity for deployment. - 可登陸地點有限 - 登陸後受人造建築阻礙，部隊開展空間受限	Terrain steepness, public highways, and buildings affect travel routes. 地形坡度、人工建造之公路與建築區，影響行進路線
Maritime weather is better from April to September, but crossing the sea in the typhoon season from July to September would affect the operations. 4-9 月海象較佳，惟 7-9 月颱風季，影響渡海行動。	- There are only 2 to 3 days per month best suited for landing. - It takes the second echelon forces 1-2 days before they can land. - 每月最適合登陸日時僅有 2-3 天 - 第二梯次部隊裝載需要 1-2 天後才能登陸	Fewer time constraints. 較無時間條件限制

In recent years, the government has vigorously promoted green energy, leading to the construction of many wind energy converters along the coast, known as wind turbines. We observe that various types of wind turbines will be built along the northern coast. Given that joint amphibious landing operations can hardly be conducted in the offshore zones where wind turbines are densely built, the enemy's actions will be thwarted, too.

值得注意的是海上人造設施近年來台灣政府大力推動綠能，台灣海峽風力強勁，是極佳的風場，我們的西部沿海也就構建了許多風力發電機組。未來的台灣海峽西部沿岸，風機的數量會越來越多，對於解放軍聯合兩棲登陸行動會造成很大的限制。

Offshore facilities—Wind turbines
海上人造設施——風機

Source 資料來源（21）

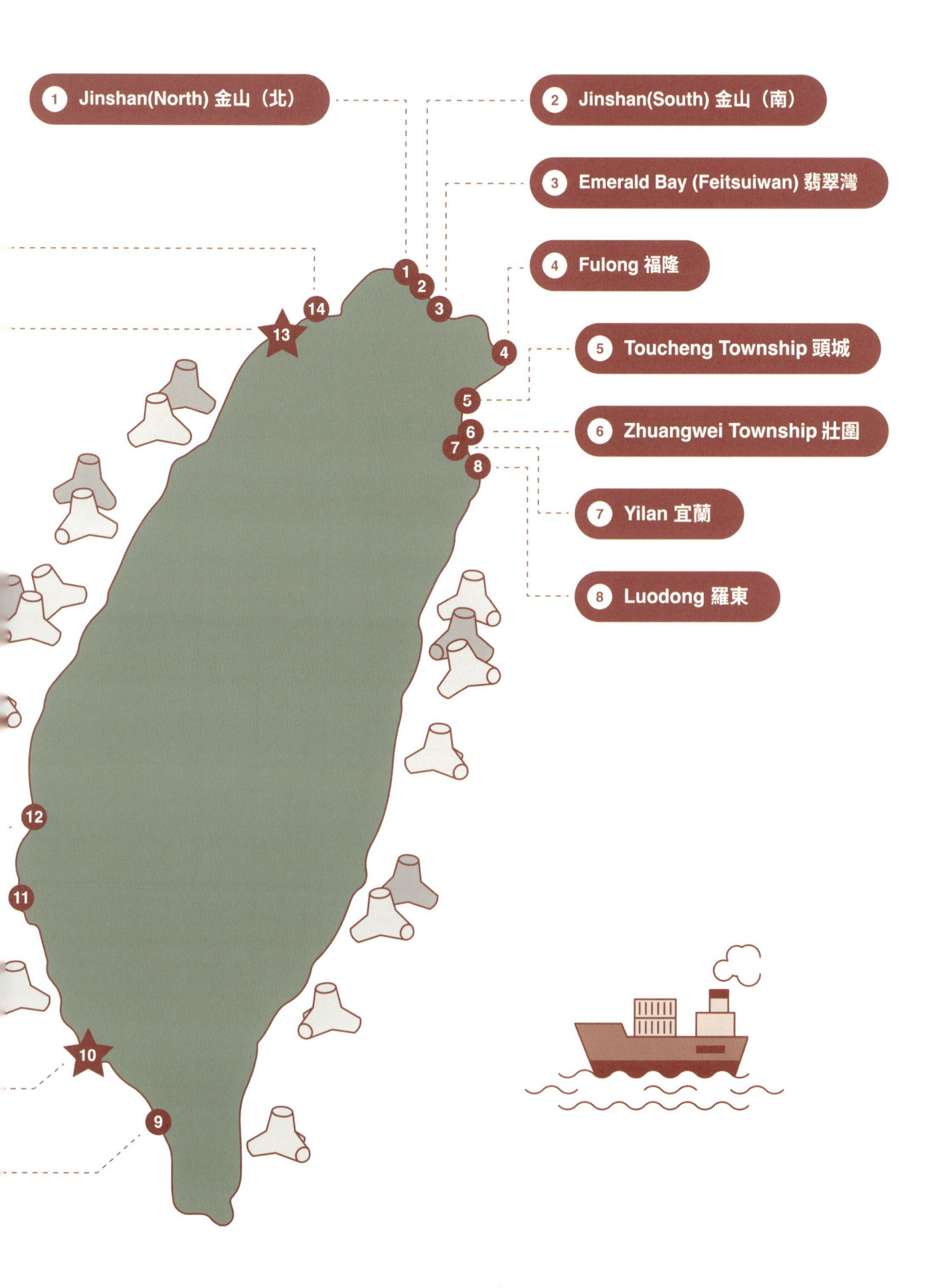

Real China: The Communist Party and the People's Liberation Army under Xi Jinping
解密中國：習近平統治下的共產黨與解放軍

① Jinshan(North) 金山（北）

② Jinshan(South) 金山（南）

③ Emerald Bay (Feitsuiwan) 翡翠灣

④ Fulong 福隆

⑤ Toucheng Township 頭城

⑥ Zhuangwei Township 壯圍

⑦ Yilan 宜蘭

⑧ Luodong 羅東

79

Taiwan's foreshore: red beach

台灣灘頭地形：紅色海灘

Red beaches refer to the beaches suitable for the PLA to conduct joint amphibious landing operations. This map shows a compilation of information collected by the Project 2049 Institute, a think tank based in Washington, D.C., on the 14 red beaches in Taiwan. Upon closely examining the map, we can see that there are fewer seawalls in eastern Taiwan, and the red beaches overlap significantly with natural beaches for a certain part of the coastline. In western Taiwan, artificial beaches have been created in most areas due to beach erosion and coastline retreat. Of the six red beaches in western Taiwan, only Luzhu Beach and Linyuan Beach can barely allow traditional joint amphibious landing operations. It would be extremely risky to conduct such landings on other beaches.

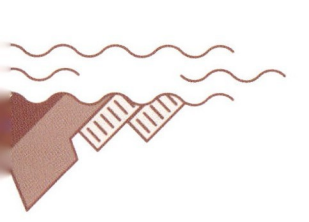

紅色海灘是指適合共軍用來實施兩棲登陸作戰的灘頭點。美國智庫於2049研究所所彙編的台灣紅色海灘圖。細看紅色海灘的進行分類表，東視的人工海岸較少，紅色海灘跟沙灘多有重疊，但西部分海岸線因海灘流失、海岸線後退，多數已建有人工海灘。因此西部的六個紅色海灘中，目前只有屬竹園流與林園的海灘，勉強可實施傳統的兩棲登陸作戰，其餘的海灘若要實施兩棲登陸作戰，將有極高風險。

- 9 Jiautang 加祿堂
- 10 Linyuan 林園
- 11 Xishu Beach 苦樹海灘
- 12 Budai Township 布袋
- 13 Luzhu District, Taoyuan 桃園蘆竹
- 14 Linkou 林口

Next, let's examine wind speed in the Taiwan Strait. The first map shows wind speed in March, with southwesterly winds blowing from south to north at force 4 on the Beaufort scale, approximately 6 meters per second. However, in December, as shown in the second map, wind speed in the Taiwan Strait reaches 13 meters per second, which is at force 7 or over on the Beaufort scale. During this time, the Taiwan Strait is extremely unsuitable for large-scale maritime navigation. Furthermore, these two maps clearly illustrate that ocean currents flow in different directions in summer and winter, which also makes large-scale maritime navigation nearly impossible in winter.

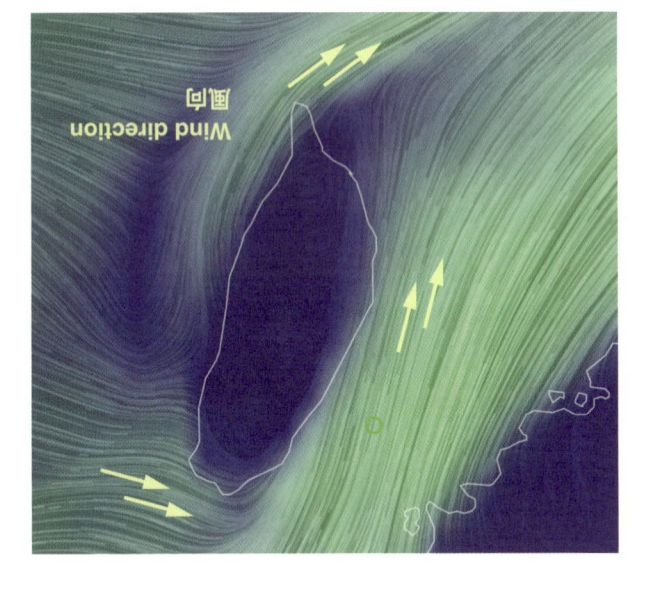

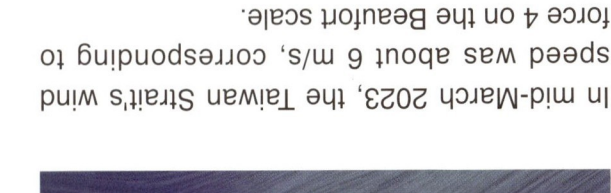

Wind speed of Taiwan's surrounding waters

In mid-March 2023, the Taiwan Strait's wind speed was about 6 m/s, corresponding to force 4 on the Beaufort scale.

In mid-December 2022, Taiwan Strait's wind speed was about 13 m/s, corresponding to force 7 on the Beaufort scale.

Source (20)

We will describe the characteristics of Taiwan's battlefield environment with a focus on hydrology, climate, and coastal terrain.

This map shows the ocean floor topography and major ocean currents around Taiwan. The blue areas indicate deeper waters, whereas the lighter areas represent shallower waters. Clearly, aside from the eastern Pacific region, most of the Taiwan Strait is shallow waters. The deep-water areas are suitable for submarine activities, whereas the shallow-water areas are suitable for mine laying. Under the circumstances, the PLA must carefully consider the potential risk arising from shallow waters before conducting large-scale maritime navigation.

以下依照水文氣候、海岸地形的重點，分別說明台灣的戰略環境特性。

我們先看台灣海況水域。圖裡顯示各種深淺的分色，水深標越深、台灣海峽大部分區域的海水深度越淺。因為潛艦只能在深水區活動，所以如果軍艦要搭載潛艦進行大規模海行動，就會受到台灣海峽的深水淺以下潛艦航行。而淺水區適合海底行動有力的護航，那就有必要評估淺水區域的軍行動的風險。

Taiwan Strait's ocean floor topography and major ocean currents
台灣海峽海底地形和主要洋流

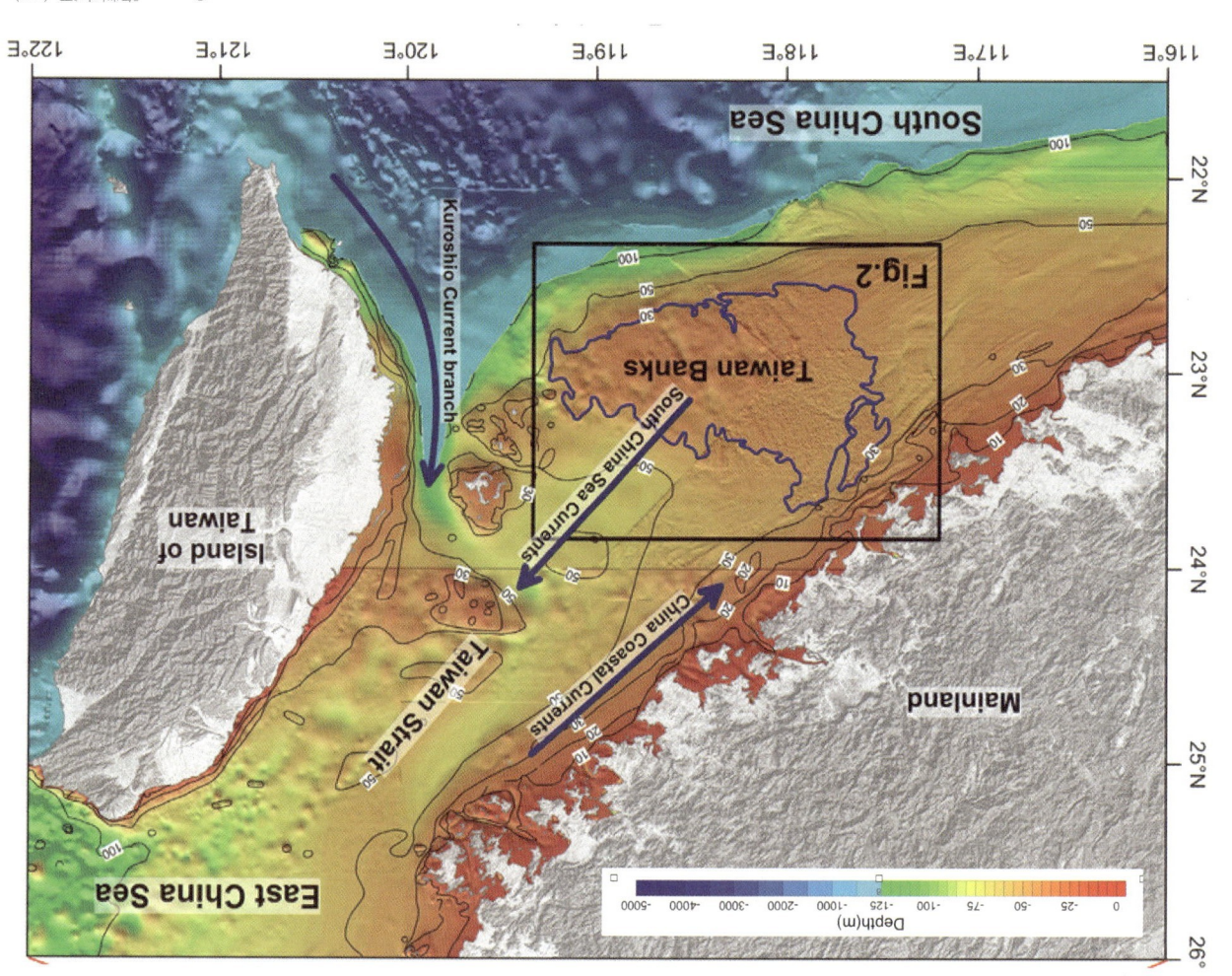

Source 資料來源 (19)

Project National Glory in 1964 (2)
1964年國光計畫（二）

This image is taken from the declassified files of Project Guoguang. Around 1964, Project Guoguang was launched to survey the weather, hydrological, and tidal conditions of the Taiwan Strait to facilitate large-scale cross-sea joint amphibious landings. This Project serves g as an example of the IPB.

The meteorological data collected and analyzed at that time included information about monsoons and typhoons and the weather conditions of months throughout a year. This map shows the weather in September and October. The green parts indicate lower wind speed (below force 4 on the Beaufort scale) whereas the red areas indicate higher wind speed at force 5 or over on the Beaufort scale. The red areas show that large-scale navigation is not advisable in a weather condition like this. Through comprehensive analysis, this chart shows that large-scale cross-sea operations are not advisable across the Taiwan Strait after mid-September.

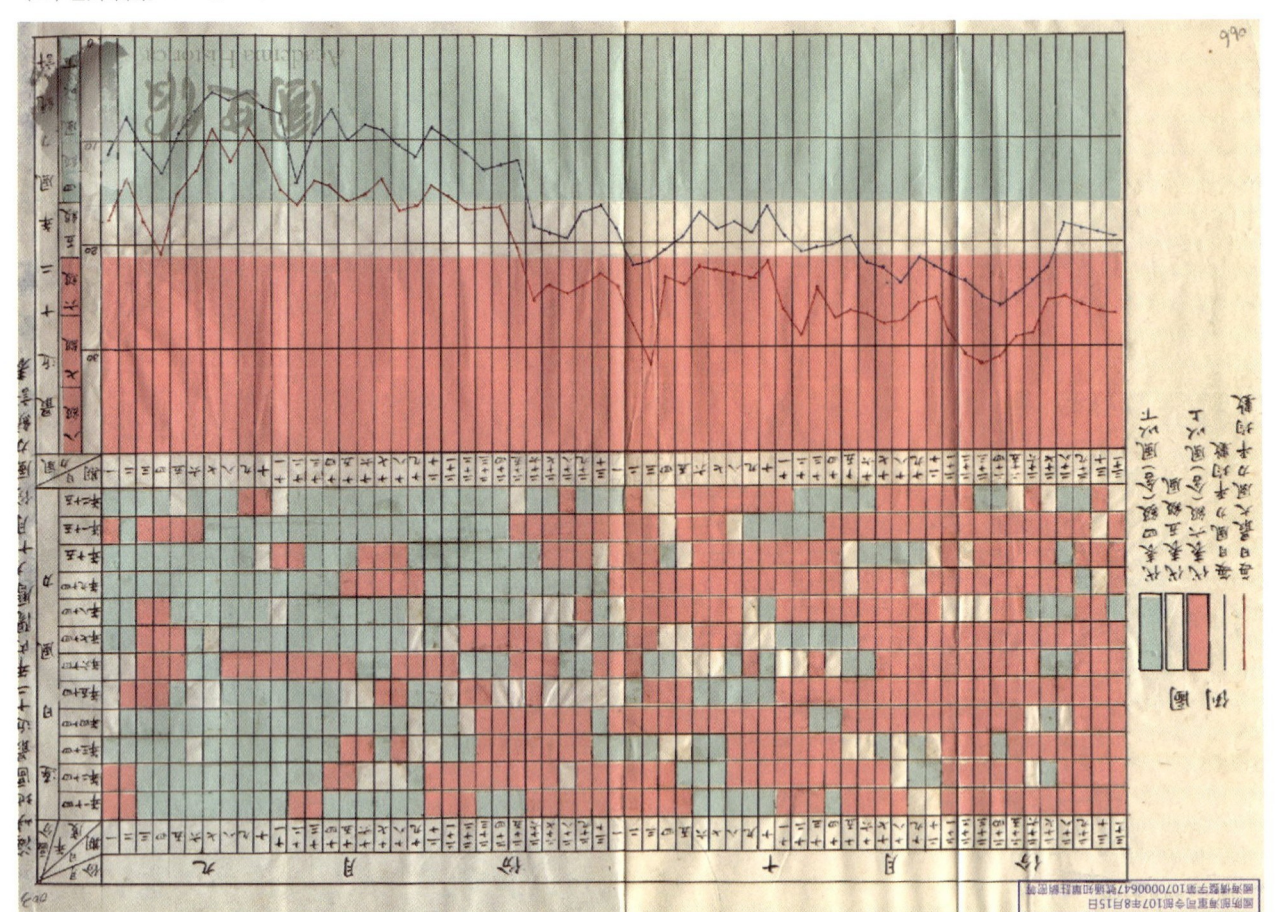

This example shows how the IPB greatly impacts our military operations.

我們用 1964 年國光計畫蒐集蒐的資料，來觀察各邊的艦艇航運時的天氣與各邊的艦艇航運時。資料中可以發現及各邊的艦艇航行時候準備信、水文、潮汐、潮流等，這都需要準備有一個參考例。

資料中可以看到，綠色邊的海象在 4 級風以下，紅色邊的海象在 5 級風以上，也就是各邊不通各大艦艇的海上航行。也就是說，各邊從 9 月中旬以後，非常不利大艦艇的渡海行動。

我這個例子就可以了解到，事先做好護情資準備，對於我後情事重行動的影響是有多重大。

Real China: The Communist Party and the People's Liberation Army under Xi Jinping
揭密中國：習近平統治下的共黨與解放軍

Source 資料來源 (18)

3-2
Taiwan's defense tactics: battlefield advantages and strategic challenges
臺灣防衛的邏輯：戰場的優勢與戰略挑戰

Characteristics of Taiwan's battlefield environment
台灣戰場環境的特徵

Next, let's have a look at the characteristics of Taiwan's battlefield environment with the steps of the IPB.

Taiwan includes the main island of Taiwan plus outlying islands, and many islets. It faces the Western Pacific to the east and the Taiwan Strait to the west. The Taiwan Strait runs approximately 370 kilometers from north to south with an average width of 180 kilometers. With that being the case, a large-scale joint island landing operation conducted by the PLA requires force and logistics projection across the Taiwan Strait. After crossing the Taiwan Strait, the PLA needs to address problems arising in island landing and land operations. Needless to say, the hydrological and meteorological conditions of the Taiwan Strait and Taiwan's coastal and topographic environment play a crucial role throughout military operations.

The hydrological, climatic, and topographic conditions of Taiwan are as follows:

The Hydrological and Climatic Conditions of Taiwan's Coast Zones

- The Taiwan Strait is a narrow and shallow channel with varying weather conditions depending on the season. The wind speed and wave heights are higher in winter and the speed of the sea current is faster in summer.

接下來，我們就依照前述準備程序，來認識台灣獨特的戰場吧！

台灣有本島、外島，以及許多離島，其隔著大陸，南北長約370公里，平均寬度約180公里。因此陸軍和黨要實施大規模登陸行動，需要經台灣海峽投射兵力和維持後勤運輸，而在登陸後，即需面臨登陸作戰的種種問題。因此，台灣海峽的水文氣象、台灣的海岸和地形環境，對整個軍事行動的重要影響不言可喻。

而台灣的水文、氣候和地形有以下特徵：

台灣海岸水文氣候

- 台灣海峽狹淺，並隨季節轉換有不同海象，冬季海峽風浪及夏季海流，皆為浪湧湍急。

台灣地形（濱海與灘岸）

- 台灣主要海灘近年來受人工建設等因素，難脫可登陸作戰範圍亦持續減少。

Taiwan's Terrain (Foreshore and backshore)

- In recent years, Taiwan's main beaches have been affected by artificial construction and changes in nature, reducing the scope of areas for landing or military operations.

The terrain of western Taiwan is low and flat and rises towards the east. Rivers on the western side flow from east to west, dividing the route from the north to the south. There are many urban settlements and highways, which affects the movement of troops.

- 臺灣西岸低平並東側漸升，南北向多河流分割，西部多城鎮化及公路，能影響部隊行動路線。

IPB procedures
戰場情報準備程序

While IPB seems incredibly difficult, we can form a clear understanding of it by reviewing its procedure and steps.

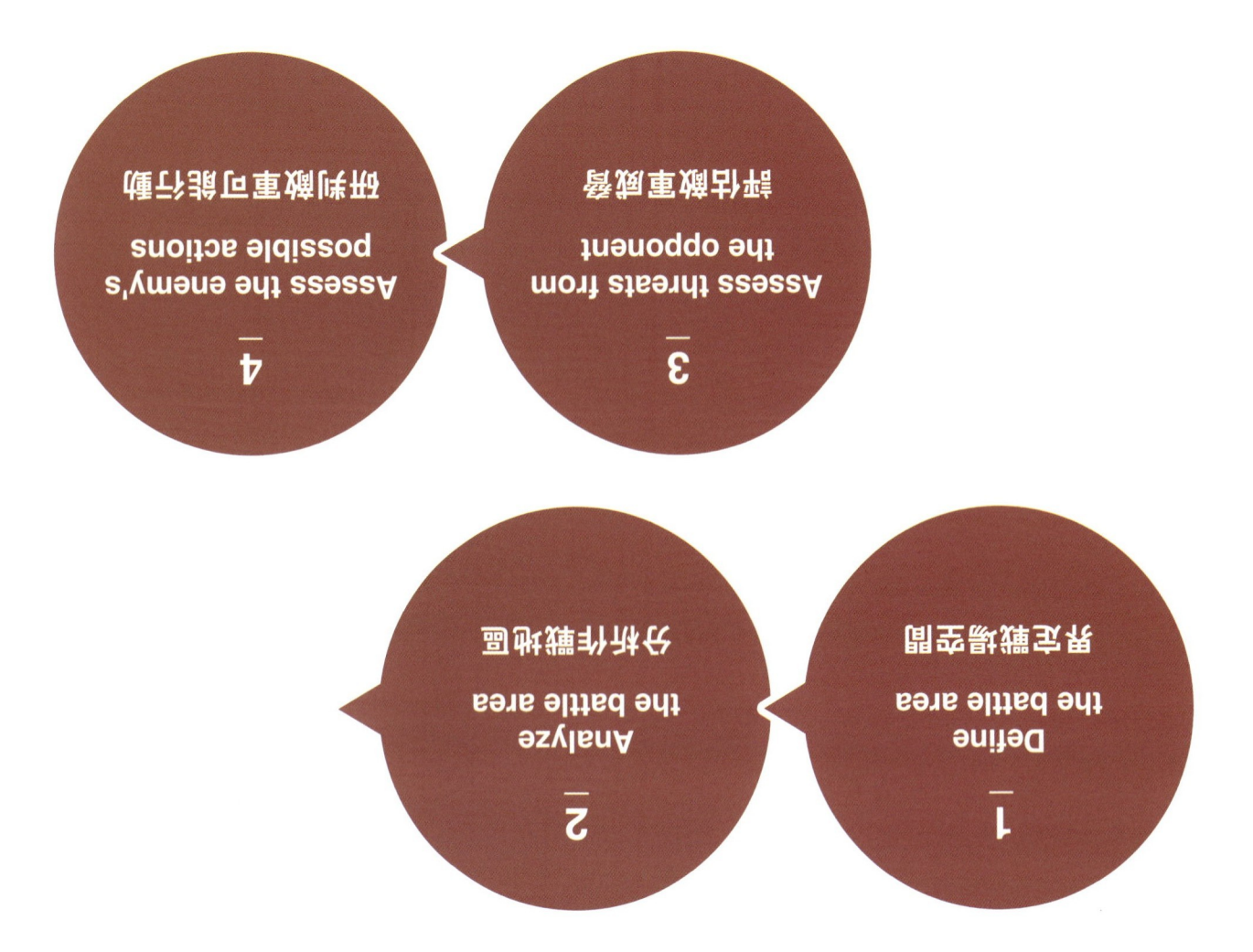

現在，就讓筆者來看看戰場情報準備程序吧！

1
Define the battle area
界定戰場空間

2
Analyze the battle area
分析作戰地區

3
Assess threats from the opponent
評估敵軍威脅

4
Assess the enemy's possible actions
研判敵軍可能行動

Purpose
目的

To familiarize troops with the battlefield environment and understand the enemy. Its ultimate goal is to analyze and understand the enemy's possible actions to anticipate the developments on the battlefield, determine what information is necessary for intelligence gathering, and collaboratively develop and evaluate our military plans with all staff members to provide commanders with points of reference when making final decisions.

「戰場情報準備」之於軍事系統「情報蒐集」還有「敵情輸入」，其最終目的即「研判敵軍可能行動」，以便在戰況發展時應變，並定要蒐集哪些資訊，且共同研擬與分析我軍行動方案，以提供指揮官下達決心之參考。

3-1
Understand your enemy, yourself, and your surroundings: intelligence preparation of the battlefield, IPB
知天知地、知己知彼：戰場情報準備

In the last unit, we will explore Taiwan's battlefield environment,and to help participants better understand the organizational structure of the PLA and its potential military operations against Taiwan while staying informed of Taiwan's self-defense capabilities so people will not be misled by false information.

在最三單元，我們要介紹台灣戰場情境，以及帶大家認識中國人民解放軍、知道解放軍有哪些行動，來增強自我防衛的信心。

What is battlefield intelligence preparation, IPB?
什麼是戰場情報準備？

We should first of all define Intelligence Preparation of the Battlefield (IPB). IPB serves as the basis for us to understand the enemy, assess threats, and predict enemy actions. Let's start with the definitions and purposes of IPB:

戰場情報準備，是掌握情報瞭解敵軍、評估威脅以及預測可能行動的主要依據，以下是戰場情報準備的定義和目的：

Definition 定義
Intelligence Preparation of the Battlefield, also known as IPB, refers to using systematic analysis due to battlefield intelligence needs to display the current weather, terrain, and enemy conditions on the battlefield through various diagrams and tables and using the previously prepared intelligence work for specific areas, such as battlefield environment analysis and enemy threat level assessment to analyze the operations the enemy could take. 戰場情報準備 (Intelligence Preparation of the Battlefield, IPB) 乃因應戰場情報需求，藉由系統的分析的方法，以各種圖表、表解方式，顯示戰場上天氣、地形、敵情概況等，針對特定地區先期完成之情報進分析與評估作業，如戰場環境分析、敵情威脅評估等，據以判斷敵可能行動之作業。

Chapter 3

Dismantle the PLA's attack plans for Taiwan: PLA's military operations against Taiwan

破解共軍攻臺策略：共軍對臺軍事行動

In 1996, during Taiwan's first direct presidential election, the CCP used missile threats against Taiwan. Before the 2024 election, Chinese military aircraft have been flying around Taiwan more frequently than ever. The likelihood of war has always been an unavoidable threat to Taiwan. However, if the CCP's PLA were to invade Taiwan, the preparations, including pre-war logistical and ammunition supplies, personnel gathering to the Eastern Theater Command, and naval landing operations, would be enormous and complex, involving first taking control of the three authorities and then occupying Taiwan. The engineering involved is massive and by no means easy.

Given that military knowledge is a highly specialized field, Radio Taiwan International (Rti) has arranged the topic: " PLA's Military Operations against Taiwan," in Unit Three and invited Li-Sheng Kuo, retired Major Geãneral of the Republic of China Army, to share military knowledge. In this unit, we will introduce the battlefield environment round Taiwan, explain the difficulties of amphibious landings, and analyze the deployment and strength of the PLA's weapons. Special attention will be given to the future production numbers of PLA aircraft and vessels. Understanding China's military knowledge is a science. Military knowledge is a science. Military knowledge is a science. Military knowledge is a science. Understanding China's military intimidation actions, avoiding unnecessary panic, and further using this knowledge to produce accurate and balanced reports and strengthen Taiwan's overall societal defense resilience are the learning objectives of this unit as planned by the Rti.

Keywords: battlefield intelligence preparation, transition from exercises to combat, airborne and heliborne operations, joint amphibious island assault

1996 年臺灣首次總統直選，中共以飛彈威脅臺灣；2024 年大選前，共機繞臺頻率達到空前的頻率，一旦臺灣無可避險的疑慮的威脅。然而，中共若放棄武裝侵略臺灣，從戰前的後勤彈藥整備、人員軍備至東部戰區，乃至兩棲渡海登陸後，先奪三權再佔領臺灣，其中工程浩大，也絕非易事。

有鑑於軍事知識是一門高深的專業，央廣在「第三單元共軍軍事行動」安排在單元三，並且邀請退役少將郭力昇先生來分享軍事知識，在本單元元，我們將介紹臺灣周邊海域諸島嶼，說明兩棲登陸作戰的困難之處，並分析中國人民解放軍武器部署與軍力分析，其中更持針對未來共軍機艦數量著墨甚多。了解一門中國的軍事力量的知識，避免不必要的恐慌，進而使用此知識，做出正確平衡的報導，強化臺灣整體社會防衛韌性，便是此單元規劃的本單元希望能達成的目標。

關鍵字：戰場情報準備、由演轉戰、空降機降作戰、聯合登陸島嶼作戰